We'll Send Ye Tae the Mars

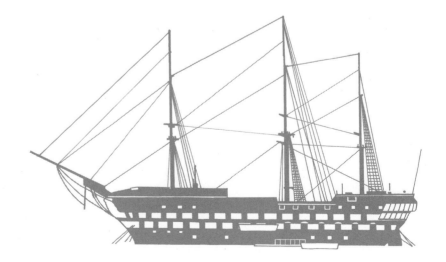

We'll Send Ye Tae the Mars

THE STORY OF DUNDEE'S LEGENDARY TRAINING SHIP

GORDON DOUGLAS

BLACK & WHITE PUBLISHING

First published 2008
by Black & White Publishing Ltd
29 Ocean Drive, Edinburgh EH6 6JL

1 3 5 7 9 10 8 6 4 2   08 09 10 11 12

ISBN: 978 1 84502 230 3

Typeset by Ellipsis Books Limited, Glasgow
Printed and bound by MPG Books Ltd, Bodmin

Dedicated to my Faither, Robert McDonald Douglas

Contents

Introduction

This book began as a musical, a strange birth for such an enterprise. I had co-written a musical with Gary Mitchell in 2006, for the Prince's Trust, which enjoyed great success at the Edinburgh Festival Fringe. The show, called *The Heart of Gold*, was one of the highlights of my somewhat varied career, and I decided to look at the possibility of a Dundee musical based on the Mars Training Ship. Once I had done some initial research, I realised that I knew less than nothing about the ship. My only memory of it was my granny's threat, whenever I was caught misbehaving: 'We'll send ye tae the Mars!' I realised that to fully understand the reasons for the necessity of such a vessel, a general knowledge of the time and place was essential. I make no apology for using many quotations from documents, books and newspaper articles, as the colour, charm and inflection are unique to the time. I make no judgement on the rights and wrongs of the institution, as I was not there, and it is neither my nor the book's ambition to do so.

As with any institution, there were good and bad boys and crew members throughout its sixty years in operation. The captain played a crucial role – Captains Wake, C. C. Scott, A. L. Scott, and Heathcote – and it may have been that these captains had different standards and codes, making the experience better under one than another. There is an obvious imbalance in the amount of time spent on each Captain Superintendent; this simply reflects the information available, and not his importance in the ship's history. The majority of the book is taken up with Charles Casely Scott's captaincy, as under his stewardship the institution was born, and grew into the legend she became.

The book is an attempt to describe how the ship came to be moored in the Tay, based on actual written or published evidence, without using conjecture, hearsay or misinformation. What I hope this will do is open the door for more information from 'Mars' families throughout the world, to encourage them to tell their stories. In conjunction with the book, there has been a website created at www.sonsofthemars.com, to list every boy who ever stepped on the ship, and in time, it will carry all the details from their admission pages.

Two of the most unusual sources for this book are the Lamb Collection, held in the Wellgate Local History Library, and the Mars Collection, to be found in the Resources Room at the Blyth Hall, Newport-on-Tay. Alexander Crawford Lamb (1843–97) collected 450 boxes of local history ephemera, including maps, photographs, books and prints, on a range of subjects, among them the Mars Training Ship. The Mars Collection, which was saved from a trip to the furnace and gifted to Fife Galleries and Museums, includes the admission and discharge books of all boys, the minute books, and a collection of contemporary newspaper cuttings relating to the ship.

I could have written three books with the amount of research I gathered in such a short time, so I have had to deal with items that I thought were particularly relevant and pertinent to the telling of the story. The photographic archive of the Mars tells its own story, and I hope that this will also create an interest in publishing more from personal family albums. The boys in the formal photos are stiff and regimented, but I must say, there weren't many smiling faces on my class photographs from school. The boys' expressions and body language in informal photographs are completely different. I hope that this will exonerate many boys who ended up on the Mars, and dispel the 'reformatory' myth; for most of them, there was simply no other place for them to go.

Thanks to all who so enthusiastically gave their time and effort to this project: McManus Gallery, Dundee City Archive, Wellgate Local History staff, D. C. Thomson, the staff at the Blyth Hall, Newport, Fife Library Service, HMS *Unicorn*, Sandy Rankine, Linda McGill, John Fitzgerald and also to my family and friends for their encouragement. Special thanks to Susan Wilson for her endless research and encouragement, and to the staff and patrons of the Phoenix Bar, Dundee, who have patiently listened to my ramblings about the Mars for the last year or two. I apologise for missing out any event that seems important to any reader, but the editing of the mass of information and the decisions about what to leave out were difficult. This is only the beginning of the story of the Mars Training Ship, not the end.

A percentage of the book's profit will go to HMS *Unicorn* to help keep her afloat. A walk round this beautifully preserved, wooden-walled vessel will give an atmosphere and feeling for the Mars experience: long may she continue to flourish. Further information and contributions may be made by contacting www.sonsofthemars.com.

1

Birth of a Notion

At sunrise all Her Majesty's ships of war moored off the dockyard, the Poictiers, 70 [guns], flag ship, hoisting the signals to dress ships – were gaily decorated with the several national and signal flags. At half-past ten o'clock the gates of the yard were thrown open for the admission of such of the public as possessed tickets.

Shortly after 12 o'clock the Lords of the Admiralty arrived. On landing they were received by Sir Thomas Bourchier, captain-superintendent of the yard, Vice Admiral Elliot, of the royal Yard at Sheerness, and Sir Gordon Bremer, the captain-superintendent of Woolwich royal dockyard. At twenty minutes to one o'clock high water was announced. Sir Thomas Bourchier was then seen leading Miss Hood, the grand-daughter of the late Captain Alexander Hood – who commanded the ship Mars in 1798, and who gloriously fell in action while engaged with French ship Hercules, of eighty guns, off the Penmarks – to the bow of the vessel; she dashed the bottle against the ship, and proclaimed her name 'Mars'.

This was the moving account from the *Morning Chronicle* of the launch of the Mars Training Ship at Chatham, on Saturday, 1 July 1848. It continues:

The next moment the huge vessel was moving, and the united bands playing 'Rule Britannia', she glided into the Medway in majestic style. She bore the royal ensign at the main, the Admiralty at the stern, and the union jack at the fore. After the ceremony, the Lords of the Admiralty, with the elite of the company, repaired to the captain superintendent's residence, and partook of a sumptuous dejeuner. Amongst the personages present were his Royal Highness the Prince de Joinville, M. Guizot, Mr Bancroft (the American Minister), Count de Jarnac, Captain and Miss Eden, Captain and Miss Charlotte Berkley, Sir Thomas and Lady Thompson, and upwards of 100 officers and ladies concerned with the garrison.

This is a most elegant birth for a magnificent ship that would spend the majority of her life moored off Woodhaven in Fife, home to over 6,000 boys. The exceptional pomp and circumstance surrounding her launch was noted at the time:

Since the launch of the Trafalgar at Woolwich no similar ceremony has excited so much attention amongst the members of the naval service as the launching of the Mars, line-of-battle ship, 82 guns, at the Royal Dockyard of this town to-day. Being the last ship of the line designed by Sir William Symonds, late surveyor of the navy, and the fact of the Lords of the Admiralty having intimated their intention of being present, gave it more than ordinary importance. We may here state that the keel of the Mars was laid down in 1840, and her dimensions are of the following extent:—

Length of gun deck 190 feet;

extreme breadth, 56 feet nine and a half inches;

depth of hold 22 feet 4 inches;

burthen in tons 2,256;

pierced for 82 guns.

The *Mars* was built as a three-masted sailing ship, a 2nd rate, two-deck, 80-gun vessel for 750 men. By the time she was launched new technology was heralding the end of sail, and so in 1855 engines were put into her, and this also happened to her eight sister ships. When she was commissioned, her only captain was James Newburgh Strange RN, son of the Chief Justice of Madras. On Wednesday, 7 March, with crew on board, the *Mars* set out for Spithead to join the Channel Fleet. During April strong winds and heavy seas led to some of the fleet's ships leaking. After inspection of the *Edgar, Algiers, Queen* and *Mars*, it was recommended that *The whole of the vessels as we have stated, are in need of repairs to both hull and machinery.*

There is little more known of the career of the *Mars* while under the captaincy of James Strange, except that in 1860 she was moved to work on the Mediterranean station. Though she now had been turned into a screw ship, by being fitted with engines, these adaptations were regarded, at best, as unsuccessful. The *Mars* was considered suitable only for coastal defence, and in 1867–9, along with many other ships, she was marked down for disposal. The Admiralty had been slow to accept the new screw design, and the

ship's creator Sir William Symonds, designer of Her Majesty's ships, was said to be utterly opposed to iron ships, describing them in his journals as *monstrous. The Times* of December 1880 carried the story of nine ships of Her Majesty's Navy which had sunk without trace since 1849, five of which had been designed by Sir William Symonds.

When she was decommissioned in 1863, she was sent to languish off Sheerness, where she would suffer the ignominy of being used as a workshop. The ship now lay neglected and uncared for, only a few miles away from where her triumphal launch had taken place fifteen years before. This would indeed have been a tragic end to this fine vessel, but she was not to die yet. Here we shall leave her till later on in this story.

Dundee in the 1860s

The population of Dundee had doubled between 1766 and 1801, to just over 26,000 inhabitants, and rocketed from then, to reach 45,355 by 1841. Conditions for all were difficult, and for the poor they were almost unbearable. The rise in population was mostly due to the economic advantages being created by employment in Dundee's growing textile trade. The explosion was fuelled by migrant workers from all over Scotland and Ireland, flocking to Dundee, creating a melting pot of ideas, religions and moralities. The gap between rich and poor had seldom been seen in such sharp focus, and living conditions for these new migrants were atrocious; while the population grew by 30,000 between 1841 and 1861, only 568 houses were built.

A report on sanitary conditions in the city was published by the British Association, in which it examines Dundee from 1867:

Figure 1 Model of the Mars Training Ship, by Mr John Allan.
(McManus Galleries, Dundee)

At this time Dundee was wholly devoid of sanitation. Drainage of even the most meagre description was barely in evidence and what there was consisted of stone built rubble, allowing the liquid to percolate through and soak into the ground, thus poisoning the soil . . . There was no proper supply of water for domestic, culinary, or flushing purposes. All there was, was largely obtained from wells situated at various places throughout the Burgh, the supply being limited and derived from springs . . . Under such conditions water closets were an impossibility. There were five such places only which came under this designation. Three were in hotels and two in private houses all of them being of a very primitive description, the flushing water having to be carried in buckets. The only other conveniences of this nature were wooden or brick privies (of which there were about 1,000), with holes sunk in the ground of from four or five feet deep under them as dung pits, into which all foul liquids were thrown. The emptying of these pits was attended with the most terrible odours. The scavengers, equipped with sea boots, started about 4 a.m. to empty them and wheeled the contents out to the streets, on which they were deposited prior to being carried away. A few of the streets in the centre of town were paved with cobble stones, while the surface of the others was of ordinary earth. The liquid spread about, formed pools, and the operation of the scavenger's broom only accentuated matters. This was the odour which met the mill and factory employees in the mornings ere they reached their work . . . The attempt to disinfect the streets and closes with chloride of lime only emphasised the nausea. The indecencies of children and others were constantly to be met with in the streets, lanes, courts, and entries owing to the inadequacy of the public accommodation of this kind.

This paints a dreadful picture of the desperation that faced the poor in Dundee. The houses and streets were a breeding ground for vermin and disease, as the report goes on to highlight:

By the census of 1871 the population had again risen to 118,977, an increase of 28,560 over that of 1861 . . . In this part [the city centre] the streets were narrow, and running off them were narrow closes, flanked on both sides by high buildings, consisting of dwellings into many of which the rays of the sun never penetrated and round which fresh air could not possibly circulate. These were largely occupied by the lowest stratum of the population. There typhus fever found a suitable habitat. Indeed this disease, which only flourishes amongst dirt, darkness, and poverty, was never absent from the City, and burst out in epidemic form from time to time with direful results . . .

In 1865–66, when the population only numbered 97,000, no fewer than 1084 cases were treated in the Infirmary, and this, of course, gives no reliable index of the number of cases in the City, as at that time there was no system of compulsory notification in force . . .

All the courts, footways, and passages in the centre of the town – of which there were about 300 – were entirely unpaved. Where there was any attempt at this it consisted of pieces of stone, bricks, or wood used as stepping stones to allow passengers in wet weather to negotiate the quagmires. These courts were also largely used for the deposit of the contents of slop pails.

Overcrowding was rampant and the staff was much too weak to cope with it energetically, inspections being carried out only between midnight and 4 a.m. Many of the buildings in the denser parts of the town were simply rotten, whilst there were between 200 and 300 underground cellars used as dwelling houses.

There was no attempt made to enforce the Smoke Abatement Act for modifying the pollution of the atmosphere by smoke emitted in dense volumes from factory stalks and which was full of smut and coom. Dairies were of the most insanitary character, being without drainage, paving, light or ventilation, or dung stances, while the milk was drawn from the cows in the most undesirable surroundings. Piggeries were numerous and scattered all over the town in undesirable places, even ben rooms, cellars, and attics being utilised as stys, the pigs mixing freely with the family . . .

Bringing up a family in the hovels, streets and closes of Dundee at this time must have been hard, and the luxuries we now take for granted, such as adequate lighting, sanitation, and clean water fit to drink, were simply daydreams to our ancestors. An analysis of the drinking water, for example, from the supply at the Ladywell (at the bottom of the Hilltown) declared that it was

nothing but a very purified sewage.

It cannot therefore be surprising that under such conditions as I have described, the most loathsome of infectious diseases were more or less constantly present in epidemic form. From the year 1860 onwards, smallpox, typhus, and typhoid or gastric fevers were serious menaces to the health of the community. In 1865 over 1000 cases of typhus came to light. For many years subsequent to this there were never less than 300 to 500 cases per annum, and the treatment of these without proper hospital accommodation other than the Royal Infirmary, which was invariably full, was a problem which the local authority long hesitated to deal with.

In the first three-quarters of the nineteenth century, conflicts such as the Franco-Prussian War, the American Civil War and the Crimean War saw a dramatic increase in demand for products made in Dundee, such as wagon covers, horse blankets, sandbags and sails. The workforce in the mills in Dundee was predominantly composed of women and young children, and the work was fast, at times dangerous, and required nimble fingers. The men who had left their farm work behind had traded honest toil for the sad streets of Dundee, and were often left out in the cold, as the womenfolk worked to feed an ever-growing family. This imbalance led to a growth in drunkenness, lawlessness and family instability. The courts and prisons were stretched to breaking point in their attempt to deal with the problems. The law dealing with orphan and abandoned children who were found wandering in Dundee's filth-ridden streets was inadequate to say the least, and throughout Britain, with industrial expansion, many started to look for answers. Whether this reforming zeal was driven by the rich to keep safe that which they had earned by the sweat of the poor, or by genuine feelings of concern for the least well off in society, is a matter for debate. There is probably truth in both.

It was obvious that the status quo could not remain. Fortunately the practice of transporting children to Australia for simple theft stopped in 1857, but in 1846 no fewer than 113 children under the age of fourteen were committed to Dundee prison. There was a growing band of reformers who seemed determined to improve the lot of the poor, and especially children. In Aberdeen, for example, Sheriff Watson had been a campaigner for change, disgusted with the number of young children who came before him convicted of petty crime. He established a Feed school in 1841, which would provide reading, writing and arithmetic: *without these he can never rise above the lowest level of society.* The children were supplied with three meals a day, while they were also taught useful trades, such as shoemaking and printing. Governor Smith, Governor of Edinburgh prison, put before the Inspector of Prisons a proposal to establish a school of industry for juvenile delinquents. Three years later he was to circulate a letter calling the attention of Edinburgh ministers and magistrates to the fact that 740 children under fourteen had been admitted to prison in the last three years.

An Edinburgh minister and champion of the poor, Dr Guthrie, had been greatly influenced by the good work he saw being done by these two men, and in 1847 he published his first plea for ragged

schools. By the end of the year Dr Guthrie's Ragged Schools had been established. Dunlop's Parliamentary Act of 1855, applying only to Scotland, conferred powers on magistrates to detain for five years in a certified industrial school any young person under the age of fourteen years found begging or not having a home. In 1852 a committee of the House of Commons was formed to inquire into the condition of criminal and destitute delinquents in the country, and to ascertain what changes were desirable in their present treatment, in order to supply industrial training, and to combine reformation with the due correction of juvenile crime. Dr Guthrie was called to give evidence, and the result was Lord Palmerston's Act of 1854, which accredited reformatories, and importantly, funded them out of public funds. This was to see a rapid growth, and in 1859 the Reformatories and Refuge Union had been formed, and a report, issued by the government inspectors appointed to visit certified Reformatory Schools and Industrial Schools, showed fourteen Reformatories and nineteen Industrial Schools in 1866 in Scotland.

The possible formation of a new institution, such as the Mars, must have sent shock waves through the many other charitable institutions in the city, which also depended on the goodwill of the populace to survive, including the Orphan Institution, the Industrial School, the Boys' Home and the Poorhouse. An article in the *Dundee Year Book 1896* looks back and explains the difference between the options:

> *In Dundee there are four agencies which directly deal with this problem of neglected children. The Orphan Institution is concerned only with what might be called the pure type of orphan – that is children who have lost their parents, but who do not come within*

the pauper class and have no criminal taint about them. In this case the problem is at its simplest. Then comes the Mars Training Ship – an institution for lads who might possibly drift into crime if left in their surroundings. Then comes the Industrial School for boys and girls, composed of those brought before the Police Court – generally on some charge. In the case of a petty theft or a crime of a similar nature the charge is 'withdrawn', and by a humane if polite fiction these children are committed to the Mars or Industrial School 'without a conviction being recorded against them'. Then there are the pauper children, with whom the Parish Council more immediately deals. These are partly located in East Poorhouse, and partly boarded out in country districts. As auxiliaries there are the Children's Shelter and the Boys' Home.

Obviously, the choice for the poor and unfortunate was not one to be envied, and the insanitary conditions and overcrowding of 'home life' meant that for most children the streets became their home. Poverty takes a heavy toll; in many cases, you lose dignity, freedom, choice, self-respect, and often most importantly, a voice. A letter by Alexander Elliot, published in the *Dundee Advertiser* of 24 January 1881, sheds some light on one of the agencies that were attempting to address the problem:

A WALK THROUGH THE COMBINATION POORHOUSE

Sir, In my last letter I referred to the treatment of the ordinary female paupers in the East End Poorhouse . . . [Mr Elliot had been shown round the poorhouse the previous Sunday, and found] flowers adorn the tables, and pictures ornament the walls. The windows are draped with red curtains, neatly fringed. Every apartment is impregnated with cheerfulness, and presents a most pleasing aspect. But why, I would ask, are the carpetings removed on a Sunday – the day of all days that should make glad the hearts of the inmates? Are they kept solely for ornament to be shown to visitors: I happened to visit these wards the following Sabbath. The carpets were rolled up, and the flowers had vanished. The signs of gladness were no longer visible. The apartments which the day before were so full of beauty were now bare, colourless and desolate. On Monday mornings, one of the assistants informed me, the scene was changed. The carpets were unrolled, the flowers replaced, and for the next six days, the paupers enjoyed their own again. The reason the lunatics have more luxuries than sane paupers is easily explained. The Government pays at the rate of 4/- per week for each lunatic, and the Parochial Board is expected to contribute an equal sum towards their maintenance . . . Of all classes of paupers, the lunatics are certainly the most comfortable, being fairly treated and fed. If I ever become an inmate of this 'house' I would like to live in the lunatic wards.

It seems an odd wish, but one based on his experience, not mine. So it would seem that the lunatics are the lucky ones in this institution, a frightening thought, is it not? Mr Elliot moves on, but not before he meets one more poor soul:

An old man with a vacant expression on his countenance sat in a quiet nook at the 'ingleside'. His story too, is a sad one. At one time he was a prosperous planter in Jamaica, he was ruined, he now lives at the expense of the parish, his wits are gone. A romance of life – in epitome!

Crossing the courtyard we were shown the workshops. The rooms of the tailors and shoemakers are very suitable for the purpose; but I have no hesitation in saying that the 'teasing room' is a disgrace to this or any other parish . . . It is 35 and a half feet long, 30 feet broad, and from 10 to 12 feet high. It is stocked with piles of ropes, teased and unteased, and yarn, wound and unwound. The antiquated pirn wheel, with the familiar 'swifts', birrs in one corner; seventeen lunatics, jabbering and teasing at the same time, occupy the other corner; whilst in the centre a group of ordinary genus homo paupers with weary fingers separate one twist of rope from another. With his back to the fire the taskmaster looks complacently on. He is monarch of all he surveys. In the midst of these poor people I espied a character well known to Dundee low life, and who for years had a habitation and a name in Fish Street and Greenmarket. Often have I listened, to his cries of 'Oringers, a penny the pund', and 'Fresh herrin and caller haddies, dirt cheap! – three a penny!' A few

days before I saw him hawking 'oringers', and was astonished at his speedy translation from the streets to the Poorhouse.

He moves on to describe conditions for the youngest children of the Poorhouse, the 'purest victims of poverty':

The room inhabited by children from three to four years of age is another exceptional sight. It would make a heart bleed to see so many little creatures – the most of whom have been 'thrown upon the parish' – neglected or abandoned. Some of them are orphans. Home have they none, except the Poorhouse! About thirty of the waifs were assembled together in a large room. A big fire, with a screen, burned cheerily in the grate. It was the only good fire I saw in the rambles; but still the room had a cold, chilly air about it, and some of the youngsters clung greedily about the fireplace. These children appeared healthy; but I could easily perceive that there was a 'waffleness' about their limbs – a want of stamina in their constitutions. Their food is the same as that of the grown-up people: porridge for breakfast, broth for dinner, porridge for supper. Porridge, in fact, appears to be the backbone of the establishment . . . Poor little outcasts of society! On leaving the room, I could scarcely keep down the big lump that arose in my throat . . .

We were conducted to the principal gateway, and were about to bid goodby [sic] to the Governor. I desired, however, to be shown into one of the outhouses adjoining. I was astonished to find it almost empty. The evening previous, in company with Councillor McKinnon, Mr James Robertson, and Mr David Gray, members of the Board, I had visited this same room, and found nineteen boys and three men employed in the universal occupation of sack-sewing. The room, besides being ill ventilated, was lighted with tallow candles, which were placed in grotesque sockets between every two of the 'labourers', whose ages ranged from twelve to thirteen years. [Later Mr Elliot corrects himself, stating that the boys were aged between eight and thirteen.] *The room was small. The little fellows plied the needle and thread with hearty goodwill. I asked the governor what had become of these boys. They were changing their clothing, he said; which was done once a fortnight. These boys, I was informed, were engaged several hours every day sewing sacks in this stifling atmosphere. Mr Skene said he himself had commenced to work early in life, and had found the advantage of it. He, therefore, believed in boy labour; so do I, but at the same time I would give them plenty of 'grub'. Fill up their platters for them. They cannot help the position in which they are placed. Do away with their watery 'waefu' faces, and you will make strong men of them. Give them a little more time for play, and the community in the long run will find the advantage of such training.*

Possibly Mr Elliot is an idealist? The management of the Poorhouse may not believe that its role is to fatten up its inmates but to keep them alive and, with meagre funding, survive itself. He sums up:

> *My impression was that the Poorhouse is a vast machine, and requires the greatest care and oversight in its regulation. No one could find fault with the prevailing cleanliness and order. But long may we be kept out of it is the wish of yours, &c.,*
>
> *Alex. Elliot*
> *Lochee, January 1881*

In a sense, this letter describes the choice that had to be made between the welfare of the poor and unfortunate and the need for financial prudence. The poor throughout Scotland had a choice – to live or die. Small children, like the rats they shared the dark lonely streets with, were being treated as something to eradicate by some sections of the community, while others saw the problem for what it was, a tragic indictment of the society which they had created.

The 'Oliver Twist case', which was featured in the pages of the *Dundee Advertiser* a few years later, exposes the hypocrisy of care, concern and cost. In this case, a small boy named William Quin, seven years of age, was brought before Baillie Cleghorn, at the Dundee Police Court, for 'disposal'. It seems that William was an illegitimate child whose father was a soldier; his mother, who had married recently and moved to Edinburgh, had abandoned the boy. His aunt had looked after him, but having become tired of the boy, she took him to the police office, and wished to leave him there. At this point, she was told to take him to Liff and Benvie Parochial Board, which she did:

Next forenoon the little fellow – shirtless, shoeless, with hardly a rag to cover him, crying pitifully from cold and hunger – came to the Police Office and stated that 'the wifie' had turned him out, and asked if they would keep him, as he had nowhere to go . . .

The court being over, he was kept there till the afternoon, when he was conveyed to the Liff and Benvie Parochial Board Office, and left there in charge of the officer. Within an hour and a half he returned to the office crying as before, and stating that they would not keep him 'in that shop', and that 'the mannie' had turned him out.

It seems strange, when they can lift a boy from the streets, that this poor wee soul can't get himself arrested! In the meantime, William is sent off to the Industrial School. The arguments rage on, both emotional and legal, for almost a month, when an application is brought by William's natural guardian, his grandfather, who asks for him to be sent to a Roman Catholic Industrial School in Glasgow. In court:

The Assessor – His mother is alive.

Mr Fay – But she has deserted him.

The Grandfather – When I was able to keep a house of my own, I cared for the boy as if he were my own. [The grandfather is now an inmate of the Poorhouse.]

Baillie Cleghorn – How long is that ago?

The Grandfather – I don't mind.

Mr Mackay – Is it ten years ago?

The Grandfather – It is not.

Mr Mackay – Well is it eight?

The Grandfather – No; the child is not that age.

The argument now seems to hinge on the child's religious persuasion, and the fact that this appeal comes after he has been in the Industrial School for over thirty days, the length of time for appeals to be heard; in fact he has been there for thirty-one days. Baillie Cleghorn, however, allows the boy to be sent to Glasgow, but not before Mr Mackie, speaking on behalf of the Industrial School, complains about the loss of the boy.

Mr Mackie – And now that we have been at the trouble of cleaning him for a month that he should be taken from us? It is very strange that this thing should crop up now. The boy was in existence before, and for months and weeks running wild outside, and no one claimed him; but now that he has been taken care of they come forward to do so.

This hardly shows a natural compassion; it seems more as if they have lost a commodity, or simply an income?

These are some examples of how some of the poor were treated in nineteenth-century Dundee, and of what they could expect from a society trying to build a system of social justice. This is the world that the Mars is slowly heading towards.

The Admiralty's search for sailors for the Royal Navy

Since the end of the Napoleonic Wars the Royal Navy's practice of press-ganging, or impressments, had been stopped, and the need for a standing body of well-drilled professional sailors was clear; but where were they to come from? In 1847 an Act of Parliament was seen as a starting point for the establishment of a formal enlistment of boys training for a career at sea. A committee on manning in 1852 endorsed the need for the effective recruitment of boys for a future, efficient, professional and permanent navy. At that time, it was estimated that 3,500 boy recruits would be needed each year.

In 1854 the first training ship for boys, HMS *Ganges*, was established. *The Scotsman* of 12 July 1859 looks at the problem:

THE NEED OF THE MOMENT: MANNING THE NAVY

(from the economist)

The real difficulty in connection with our coast defences and the increase of our naval power, lies not in our ability to build ships, but to man them . . .

What is the position of the Royal Navy with regard to manning? . . .

The Admiralty must devise some better and more reliable system. The service must be made one in itself more attractive; but most of all it will be needful that a supply for the Royal Navy must be raised by an enlarged system of entering and training youths, and by keeping under some well-regulated system a permanent reserve of men. In short, our navy must become a service, and less a precarious and accidental source of employment. We rear, and train, and keep a standing army. Under modifications, but based upon the same principle, we must train and keep a standing reserve for our navy.

Much later, an article appeared in *The Scotsman* looking back at the old training ships, which explains the reasoning behind the decision to establish Industrial Training ships such as the Mars:

The establishment of these training ships and the discarding of wooden ships by the Royal Navy stand almost in the relation of cause and effect. In the '60's public attention was directed to the large percentage of foreigners in British merchant crews, and it was insinuated that the reason lay partly in the inferior type of Britons offering themselves as seamen. The remedy enthusiastically taken up was training ships for boys, and it so happened that the Navy had a huge stock of wooden ships, in many cases not ten years old, which it was very glad to sell or lend to private persons or committees for training purposes, so that the majority of these ships were vessels built long after the French wars, and had seen no active service.

Was this the signal that the great and the good in Dundee were looking for? Was this a way of killing two birds with one stone? A self-financing home for homeless and destitute boys, and a training institution, both under one roof? The demand for young sailors for the Royal Navy and Merchant Service was obvious, and it appeared that the Navy would accept the right boys. As they were to find out, the naval authorities did not view boys from all training ships in the same light – there were training ship boys and 'industrial' training ship boys.

Applications were made to the Admiralty from all over Britain for the loan of these redundant wooden ships. A letter from George Armistead and William Hay, Dundee's Lord Provost at the time, to the Chief Magistrate and Harbour Board explains a little of their confidence and background:

Dundee 15th January 1869

Dear Sir, Since we have had the prospect of a considerable reduction in our Naval Establishment, I have thought this a good opportunity to get a ship stationed in the Firth of Tay, and accordingly have felt my way on the subject by communicating with the Admiralty. I am given to understand that there would be no difficulty in that department, but that the right course is to memorialise the home office. Of course, this must be done by the proper legal authorities here, and I therefore address you, as Chief Magistrate and Chairman of the Harbour Board, drawing your attention to the subject, in order that you may take steps as you may think right in the matter.

I also address the Chairman of the Chamber of Commerce on the subject . . .

I am your obedient servant

Geo. Armistead
William Hay Esq., Provost of Dundee

Dundee was very fortunate that a Dundonian, the MP for Montrose Burghs, W. E. Baxter, was Secretary of the Admiralty at the time, and he may have helped sway decisions in Dundee's favour as regards a ship for the Tay. A letter was received by William Hay from Mr Baxter laying down the ground rules, should an appropriate ship be found to 'loan' to the City.

Admiralty, 26th January 1869

Sir,

I have received and laid before my Lords Commissioners of the Admiralty the Memorial signed by you on behalf of the Trustees of the Harbour of Dundee and which has been forwarded to this office by the Secretary of State for the Home Department, in regard to the proposal to station a training ship on the River Tay, so that youths could be brought forward and qualified for the Service, either in the navy or mercantile marine of the Empire . . .

This seems a most satisfactory first step in the acquisition of a vessel fit for the purpose, but the rest of the letter states quite categorically that there will be no funding by the Admiralty, beyond the lending of the ship:

It must be understood however, that after receiving the information requested, their Lordships will consult with the Lords Commissioners of the Treasury on the matter, and that it must in any case be a stipulation that the ship required can only be lent to the Society, and that their Lordships will not incur any expense whatever, on account of such a loan, even if they should be enabled to comply with the application of the Memorialists.

I am, Sir,

Your Obedient Servant

W. E. Baxter

It seems perfectly clear that the Admiralty, while seemingly in favour of the training ship plan, has immediately distanced itself from any responsibility for its maintenance. It does beg the question of whether they were simply disposing of old ships for the public good and conscience, or whether they saw this as a strategic tool to improve and increase the standard of young men needed for the Royal Navy and Mercantile Service. No doubt buoyed by this success, an advert appears in the local newspapers with the headline:

TRAINING SHIP FOR THE TAY

It will be seen that a public meeting is to be held in the town hall, Dundee on Thursday next for the purpose of forming an Association, to take charge of the Training Ship.

On 25 March 1869 the meeting took place attended by all the great and the good of Dundee, and under the chairmanship of Provost Hay, Mr Thomas Couper moved the following resolution:

That the following noblemen and gentlemen be the Patrons, General and Executive Committees for the management of the Institution:–

Patrons – Right Hon. Earl Dalhousie; Right Hon. Lord Kinnaird; Right Hon. Earl of Camperdown; Right Hon. Earl of Strathmore; Sir J. Ogilvy, Bart.,

M.P.; Sir David Baxter, Bart.; Edward Baxter, Esq., of Kincaldrum; George Armistead, Esq., M.P.; W. E. Baxter, Esq., M.P.; the Hon. Charles Carnegie, M.P.; the Hon. Arthur Kinnaird, M.P.; C. S. Parker, Esq., M.P.; Sir R. Anstruther, M.P.; Edward Ellice, M.P.; G. Robertson Chaplin, Esq. of Colliston.

President of the Institution – Francis Molison, Esq. Chairman of Committees – W. W. Renny, Esq. General Committee – Sheriff-Substitutes at Forfar, Perth, Dundee, Cupar Fife; Provosts of Dundee, Arbroath, Montrose, Brechin, Forfar, Perth, St Andrews, Cupar Fife; Messrs. Alex. Anderson, Patrick Anderson, Thomas Bell, Alex. Buist, Charles Clarke, Thomas Couper, James Cox, William Cox, James Cunningham, W. O. Dalgleish, W. G. Don, Gershom Gourlay, Joseph Grimond, John Leng, William Lowson, Robert McKenzie, D. O. Dalgleish, Captain Maitland Dougall, R.N., James Ramsay jr., W. W. Renny, George Rough, Frank Sandeman, John Sharp, William Small, Thomas Smith, A. Traill, George Burnett, Pat. Watson, Henry B. Ferguson, John Kirkland and John Gordon – with power to add.

Executive Committee – Thomas Couper, W. W. Renny, Captain Maitland Dougall, R.N., Captain J. O. Dalgleish, R.N., R. McKenzie, James Ramsay, jr., Thomas Smith, A. Traill, George Burnett, George Rough, Thomas Bell. Secretary and Treasurer – George Jack ex-officio.

Mr George Jack, Secretary to the local Marine Board,

was, on the motion of Mr A. J. Buist, appointed Secretary for the meeting.

As admirable a collection of fine gentlemen as you could wish for, at the birth of such an institution, as yet unnamed. Mr Burnett begins by describing the reality and potential, as he sees it, for the training ship:

Mr George Burnett, who rose amid applause, said – Mr Provost and Gentlemen, – I have been asked to state what I have seen in visiting some of the reformatory and training ships stationed at different places throughout the country; and I am sure it will require no endeavour on my part to make it patent to you all how many objects there are in the shape of destitute boys deprived of their parents, or otherwise in such circumstances as to be in need of the institution we are about to establish. They are found in our streets, not only here – more especially at present, in consequence of the depressed state of our staple trade – but also in the neighbouring towns, and in many parts of the county. And we don't intend this institution to be for Dundee alone. We intend it to be for the whole district of country surrounding the Tay. We will be very glad to receive boys from other counties; and I have no doubt that gentlemen connected to the counties will take the opportunity of recommending to us proper objects for this charity.

Mr Burnett proceeds to examine the need for boys to be prepared for life in the Royal Navy and Merchant Service, and describes the different types of ships he has visited, ending with the type proposed for the Tay:

. . . it is nothing more or less than an industrial school afloat. We are indebted entirely for the permission of the Government to carry out this system of an industrial school afloat to Mr James Hall, of Newcastle, who has, by his perseverance and energy and benevolence, induced the Government to sanction the system.

. . . I would just point out that this vessel, you will see, would be a valuable adjunct, not only to the Industrial Schools already existing, but also to the Orphan Institution, where there are boys, who, when their time is up at these institutions desire to go to sea. The boys sent on board this training ship are paid for by Government to the extent of 5/- a head per week, making it £13 10/- per annum. It is a strange anomaly that while Government gives only 5/- a week for the boys sent on board this ship, they give 6/- per head a week for those sent on board reformatory ships . . .

It was an enthusiastic speech by Mr Burnett, who saw a bright future for the institution, but what of the magistrates? Next to speak was a very straight-talking Sheriff Smith, who pointed out that the children were not the authors of their own misfortune:

Sheriff Smith – It seems to me there are two ways of looking at this question. The one is how to procure a supply of seamen for the navy, and the other is how to get rid of juvenile delinquents with whom our town is infested!

. . . It is simply that these helpless little ones – who have either no parents at all, or, if they have a surviving parent, a person so worthless and so abandoned as to be in every sense worse than none – are entitled to come forward and demand that society shall take the place of the parent, and do its best to train them up to be useful citizens. I think an appeal of that kind made to the rich and prosperous in a great community such as this would fall upon no inattentive ear. I can hardly imagine a claim upon public benevolence which would enlist so powerfully the best feelings and the best sympathies of every right-minded person. Because these unfortunate children are not the authors of their own misfortune; they are in some instances the offspring of the thriftless, the drunken, the profligate, or it may be that they are deprived by death of the only person who can attend to their upbringing.

The sheriff's disquiet in his speech seems to focus not on the delinquent children, but on the parents and the situation in which they find themselves. As he explains:

It seems to me the creation of a class of this kind is one of the necessary conditions of the existence of large towns, and therefore the duty of caring for them is a duty of the highest moral and social obligation, which no community, if it expects the blessing of Divine Providence, is entitled to decline. I do not say it is a charity claimable only from the rich and prosperous, but a social obligation towards which every person is bound to contribute to the extent of his ability. Therefore, it is clear to me that a movement of this kind is one which must command itself to every kind person. (Hear, hear.)

Stirring stuff by Sheriff Smith, but he is not finished yet, not by a long way; he continues in magnificently Dickensian style:

But I am not going to defend it, or put it forward on any such high grounds as these. We are a commercial people, accustomed to sum up a balance-sheet as well as most men. I will, therefore, simply place before you a debtor and creditor account between these children on the one hand and society on the other, in order to show you what will be the result if you do nothing, and what will certainly be the consequence if you interfere in the way proposed. On the first hypothesis, the child left to himself naturally takes to stealing. He must live somehow. He is trained to nothing; he has no education; he has not a particle of religion; and therefore, in order to live, he must almost necessarily steal. Conviction follows conviction till he soon sinks into the category of the habitual criminal – a thief by profession – the natural enemy of all organised society – and ends his career with a long term of penal servitude. When society comes to reckon up its account with him, it finds it has got a bad bargain indeed. What with policemen to look after him, building jails to hold him, and the expense of keeping him there, he has cost a very large sum of money. That is the effect of doing nothing. On the other hand, if you come forward and in the name of society take him by the collar – kindly of course, but at the same time in a rather firm and determined manner – and clothe him and feed him and train him to some useful occupation, instead of proving a pest, he will be an advantage to society. (Applause.)

I reproduce this speech at length, as I believe it shows an interesting attitude to the problems that they faced, and that we face even to this day. Whether the solution was the best or most appropriate, I prefer to leave to the experts. The speech does give a unique insight into one man's thinking at the time, and he continues:

I need not say, of course, that to a large extent the success of the enterprise will be in the hands of Police Magistrates; and I need not remind gentlemen of their judicial experience that there can be no greater mistake in dealing with juvenile delinquents than to give way to momentary feelings of compassion and leniency. It is very hard, no doubt, to resist the tears of a boy or the entreaties of a mother, but they must remember that in pronouncing orders under the Act of Parliament, they are not intended as a punishment to the boy, but as a measure designed by the State for his own good. (Applause.)

Nothing can be said in favour of a practice, of which I have seen some evidence, of dismissing a boy with an almost nominal term of imprisonment, or perhaps a slight corporal chastisement. I believe in nine cases out of ten the boy goes out of the hands of the police worse than when he came in. He goes forth to

society with the jail brand upon him. He has elected his course in life, and soon sinks into the category of the regular jail bird. The better course seems to me to be that if the boy is in possession of any parent who is disposed to look after him and attend to his upbringing, he should be dismissed without any punishment at all for the first or second offence, so as to give him one more chance of an honest livelihood; but if there is no person who can be fairly trusted with this duty his career should be cut short at once, either by sending him to a Reformatory or to an Industrial School.

. . . I therefore, for the reasons I have stated, move –

'That the meeting, recognising the desirability of additional education for poor and destitute boys, and the necessity that exists for an increased supply of seamen, resolve that a Training Ship Institution be formed, to be called, after the name of the vessel so obtained "The . . . Training Ship Institution for Boys in the River Tay".'

. . . Mr Couper concluded by remarking that he concurred in the proposal that the ship should be an Industrial Training School – not so much for lads already tainted with crime, as for those on the verge of ruin . . .

Figure 2 This is thought to be one of the earliest views of the Mars, taken from west Wormit, showing the church spires and smoke stacks of Dundee in the background.
(University of Dundee Archive Services)

The Rev. Dr Watson moved as follows:

'That the Executive Committee be empowered to collect subscriptions for the outfit of the vessel and the supplementing of the income; that they be empowered to frame a constitution for the management of the Institution, and submit it to the General Committee for approval; that they be empowered to get a vessel from the Admiralty, on the best terms they can as regards stores and equipment, to make the necessary arrangements for bringing the ship to the Tay, to appoint the necessary staff for the management of the ship, and in general to make all arrangements for carrying out the objects of the Institution.'

As we wait for news of the ship we are to be offered, the like-minded philanthropists in Edinburgh hold their breath, and wait to find out if their application to the Admiralty will bear fruit. It would appear that should they be granted a ship, they intend to use it as a Reformatory Ship. The Captain of the Wellesley Training Ship wrote an interesting letter to *The Scotsman*, which was reprinted in the *Dundee Advertiser* on Friday, 2 April 1869:

Commander Pocock, R.N., Superintendent of the Wellesley Training Ship on the Tyne, writes strongly to The Scotsman against a proposal to have a Reformatory Ship on the Forth, and recommending an Industrial Training Ship as is proposed on the Tay. In the course of his letter he says:–

The Industrial Schools Act of 1866 entitles the managers to 5/- a head per week, this ship now receives 6/-, the same as Reformatories, but still we are worse off, for they have an allowance of 1/- or 2/- a week from jails. The last returns as follows:–

	Boys	Government allowance	Jails	Subscriptions
Cornwall	283	£3,274	£1,071	£198
Akbar	216	£2,600	£482	—
Clarence	209	£3,178	£592	£195

There is, however, I believe, a bill now before Parliament which, if it becomes law, will put Industrial Schools on a better footing, and it is to be hoped that soon the prevention of crime will at least be as highly subsidised as the reformation of criminals.

I wonder how many agencies working in the field today could echo these words? Captain Pocock continues to give his message a personal touch, the sentiments of which seem to echo throughout this book:

Before coming here, I was told that I should find the boys sent to an Industrial School, if anything, worse than those sent to a Reformatory, as the law would lay hold on those who are criminal, but too clever to be found out. That is not so; but if it were, the fact of having a single convicted criminal would deprive us of a moral influence compared with which all law and force are worthless. I could not have taken for granted that they were all perfectly truthful and honest, nor could I have told them when it was reported that the 'Wellesley' was a prison, and they were criminals, to go on shore, and by their conduct prove that it was false, and then turn them adrift on the streets of Newcastle for a couple of hours, and ever since send them on duty with money, and orders to bring back the change. For instance, I have taken out a half sovereign, 'Look here, lad. Can I trust you with that?'

'Yes Sir.'

'Of course I can.'

He gets his orders and goes off, nearly bursting with a new sense of being honest. Worldly wisdom would call this reckless. I confess I began in fear and trembling, but, on reflection, concluded I had no right to take for granted that the poor, beaten, starved beggar was worse than myself, and possibly the Righteous Judgement that judges not according to appearances would be in his favour.

Pure *Oliver Twist*, but could the Dundee Training Ship live up to such high ideals, or would it become a tyrannical place where generations of children, long after its end, would still be threatened with 'We'll send ye tae the Mars!'?

An anecdote of the time from the *Piper o' Dundee*

Overheard in Maxwelltown

Urchin of 7 (pointing across the Tay) – 'Man, Wully, I wid like fine tae be on the Mars.'

Urchin of 6 – 'So wad I, come awa, we'll stale somethin'.'

2

The Arrival of the Mars

On 22 May 1869 W. E. Baxter announced the decision to create an Industrial Training Ship on the Tay. (Mr Baxter was to relate in 1880: *It was my happy fate, as Secretary to the Admiralty at the time, to go down to Sheerness and choose the vessel for the Tay.*) The financial implications of what they had managed to achieve must have seemed daunting, and a campaign to fund the refitting of the abandoned ship was begun in earnest. At Sheerness, the Mars was remasted and fully rigged for her new career, but not repainted nor refitted, and as she had been used as a workshop since being decommissioned in 1863, she must now have been in quite a sorry state.

Things had moved swiftly since the announcement of the imminent arrival of the Mars on the Tay. Here are some of the rules and regulations drawn up for the management of the ship:

> *1. – The Institution shall be called 'The "Mars" Training Ship Institution in the River Tay for Homeless and Destitute Boys'.*
>
> *2. – The object of the Institution shall be the reception and training of boys who, through poverty, parental neglect, or from any other cause, are destitute and homeless, and in danger from the association with vice and crime. Such boys may be admitted, fed and clothed, either under powers of the Industrial Schools Act, 1866, or otherwise, as the Executive Committee determine.*
>
> *17. – The period during which a boy may remain on board Ship, and the date he is to leave it, shall be determined by the Executive Committee, subject in the case of boys discharged under the Industrial Schools Act to the consent of the Secretary of State.*

These are a few of the by-laws for the Management of the Ship, by the Executive Committee:

> *2. – The Captain shall live on board, and have sole charge of the Vessel entrusted to his care, and shall see all officers on board rightly discharge their duties. He shall also carry out efficiently all orders given to him by the Executive Committee.*
>
> *He shall be responsible to the Executive Committee for the good government of the Ship, and for the due execution of all regulations pertaining to it. While enforcing such strict discipline, he shall endeavour to gain a salutary influence over the boys individually; and, by instilling into them Christian principles, to fit them for leading a life of duty and usefulness.*
>
> *5. – The Captain shall have power to punish boys under his charge by deprivation of privileges or by the degradation from their place in the Vessel, by*

solitary confinement, or by partial stoppage of rations, or by corporal punishment; but such corporal punishment shall not exceed eighteen strokes with a birch or cane, which the Executive Committee, in extreme cases, shall have power to direct to be increased to twenty-four strokes. No corporal punishment shall be inflicted except in the presence, and by order, of the Captain.

Every boy in confinement shall receive half-a-pound of bread and either gruel or milk and water twice a day; for boys not in confinement the food shall not be partially stopped for two meals successively. No boy shall be kept in confinement for more than three days, except by a special order of the visiting members of the Committee.

These rules seem harsh for wee boys, and in the hands of a cruel captain, life on board could have been terrifying. The concept of preparing these boys for a life in the Navy or Merchant Service meant that strict discipline was essential, and these rules were in line with naval regulations. As Admiral of the Fleet, Lord Fisher recalls in his *Memories and Records*:

When I joined the Navy, in 1854, the last of Nelson's Captains was the Admiral at Plymouth. The chief object in those days seemed to be, not to keep your vessel efficient for fighting, but to keep the deck as white as snow and all the ropes taut. We midshipmen were allowed only a basin of water to wash in and the basin was inside one's sea-chest; and if anyone spilt a drop of water on the deck he was made to

holy-stone himself [holy-stone is soft sandstone used by seamen for cleaning the decks of ships].

There were many brutalities when I first entered the navy – now mercifully no more. For instance, the day I joined as a little boy I saw eight men flogged – and I fainted at the sight.

The role of captain was crucial to the success of the Training Ship, and in a newspaper article, most likely the *Dundee Advertiser*, from the Lamb Collection, it seemed that they had their man:

APPOINTMENT OF COMMANDER OF THE TAY TRAINING SHIP

Information has been received from the Admiralty that H.M.S. Mars will be rigged and ready to be towed round from Sheerness to Dundee on the 16th of July [she didn't actually arrive until 17 August]. *The Committee have made a satisfactory arrangement with the Admiralty for her being towed to the Tay. A most satisfactory appointment has been made to the command of the Ship. There were forty applications for the post. After the most careful consideration, it was unanimously resolved to appoint Captain Baldwin Arden Wake, R.N. This gentleman is in his 55th year. When a young officer on board H.M.S. Racehorse, commanded by Sir Everard Home, he was slightly wounded, and rendered distinguished service in the defence of the city of Para, in Brazil, saving by an act of gallantry a large number of Brazilian officers and men who were shut up in the*

Customhouse, and closely surrounded by an enemy who gave no quarter. He afterwards saw service in different parts of the world, and won from Lord Auckland, when First Lord of the Admiralty, the praise of being 'one of the good and hard-working officers of the Navy'. Vice Admiral Sir Charles Paget and Sir Richard Grant have also spoken in high terms of his conduct in the profession . . .

He was for some time engaged as Inspecting Commander in the Coastguard service in Cornwall, and won golden opinions for his zeal and efficiency, especially in bringing to justice a number of wreckers who plundered even dead bodies cast ashore on the Cornish Coast. Some time ago he took the temporary command of the Akbar School Frigate, under the Liverpool Reformatory Association, who made him a handsome present, 'as an acknowledgment of their appreciation of his zealous service, and of his interest and exertions on behalf of the boys'. The Committee have been highly fortunate in securing as Commander of the Training Ship an efficient officer, who is not a mere disciplinarian, but who has for a number of years taken a warm personal interest in such Institutions as he is now to be connected with.

On the face of it, the 55-year-old Captain Wake seems ideally suited to the post, as his record shows, in J. K. Nesbitt's account from the *Daily Colonist* (Victoria, British Columbia), June 1950:

He was the son of Baldwin Wake, M.D., and the grandson of Drury Wake of Coutreenhall,

Northamptonshire. [He] entered the Navy in 1827, as a first class volunteer on board the Espoir, and was employed for some time at the Cape of Good Hope. He afterwards joined the Falcon on the West Indian Station, and subsequently served on the Forester, also the San Josef and the Racehorse. He was promoted to the rank of commander in 1849 and became a captain in the retired list in 1866.

There are further deeds of derring-do listed here from the *Army and Navy Gazette*:

On the 1st of September 1830 when he was only 17 he saved John Williams, a seaman, who fell overboard from H.M. ship Falcon into the Atlantic . . . In December 1831 he saved James Ash, a seaman, who had fallen overboard in a state of intoxification. On February 13th 1833 in a storm at the Scilly Isles he saved H.M. ship Forester and all on board by taking a line on shore. In April 1834 he saved a seaman of H.M.S. Racehorse who fell from the rigging and was fast sinking. In 1836 at the insurrection of Pavia [sic] he saved 220 Brazilians by landing at night on the enemy's ground and bringing them off in boats of the Racehorse. He also saved the life of Mr Hepburn, Master Attendant, who fell into the docks at Portsmouth. He assisted Mr Ridsdale to save the life of a young man who was bathing in the Nile and was nearly lost in doing so.

The Committee must have felt that they had got the best man possible for the crucial role of Captain Superintendent of the Mars –

gallant, honourable, brave – yet they were to remove him from his post before a year had been served.

We'll return to his sad demise later. In August 1869 the newspapers marked the imminent arrival of the ship from Sheerness:

To the Editor of the Dundee Advertiser

Sir, As I have had many enquiries about the 'Mars' since my arrival to-day, I beg to make the following report:–

I passed her yesterday at 11 a.m. at anchor in Grimsby Roads, the wind fresh at north; but, as the wind died away and veered to the west through the night, it is very probable she would leave the Humber to-day.

David Johnston, master s.s. Eagle
Dundee Aug. 15 1869

The arrival of such a massive ship as the Mars in the Tay was awaited by all in Dundee and the surrounding districts with great excitement and anticipation. She arrived at the mouth of the Tay on the forenoon of 17 August. (She had been held up by gales on her way from Sheerness, in tow of the gunboat *Medusa*, and was obliged to make for Grimsby until the gale abated.)

On Tuesday forenoon, the Mars which had been procured from the Government as a training-ship for the Tay, and which had been expected for the last three or four weeks, arrived in the harbour . . .

She was easily distinguished through a glass from Dundee when at the mouth of the river, and the news of her arrival spread through the town with great rapidity. She entered the Tay between twelve and one o'clock, but as the tide was ebbing she was towed up very slowly. About three o'clock she was off Broughty Ferry, and dropped anchor in Carolina Roads about four o'clock . . .

The Mars is the largest vessel and the noblest in appearance that has ever entered the river Tay . . . at an early period of the forenoon, in the tow of the Medusa, she arrived off Broughty Castle, it appeared as if the whole of these communities had turned out to see her . . . it was noticed that Captain Dougall of Scotscraig had hoisted his flag on the top of Hill Tower, while on the northern bank of Tay a flag was also hoisted on the tower of Mr George Gillroy's splendid new mansion . . .

As she has not been painted for eight years, her hull looks anything but smart at present, but the paint brush will soon make a great difference in her appearance.

When Mr Burnett visited her at Sheerness, on behalf of the Training Ship subscribers, she was a mere hulk, without masts, rigging, or fittings of any kind, but since then, owing to his representations, she has been fitted up with the proper complement of masts, and with all the necessary rigging.

The ship was then anchored for the night, and the crew on board were entertained by a visit from the Fenella Aquatic Club to serenade them for a time.

The 'big ship' drew thousands to the Marine Parade in the evening, and, it being clear and calm, numerous pleasure boats made a trip round the vessel. The Pride o' the Tay was also on duty, and was largely taken advantage of . . . The Fenella Aquatic Club and a few lady friends performed a graceful act of courtesy and attention to the crew of the Mars on the night of their arrival, by serenading them from their beautiful six-oared gig. Amongst other songs special mention must be made of 'The New-England Hymn', 'Rule Britannia', and 'God Save the Queen'. The crew of the Mars joined in the chorus of 'Rule Britannia', and, with their full and well-trained voices, aided the proper rendering of this inspiriting song . . . More songs were asked by the crew; but as several of the members had to leave by train for Carnoustie, 'Good Nights' were exchanged, with a promise to return some other evening.

An interesting historical footnote of another kind comes from an article describing her arrival in the river, in the *Dundee Advertiser*, 20 August 1869:

Already the photographic art has been employed upon the Mars, for as she passed Broughty Ferry on Tuesday she was photographed by Mr Cormack Brown, and we were shown specimens of the photographs in Dundee on Tuesday evening, in which her enormous bulk, as seen from the shore, completely dwarfs all the vessels beside her. The photograph is very creditable to Mr Brown.

Alexander McDougall, the ship's carpenter, takes up the story of her mooring, in an interview given by him on his retiral from the ship:

The following day Captain Taylor, then Pilotmaster, took her up the Tay, and moored her in mid-stream opposite Woodhaven. She was moored with two anchors and a swivel, so that she swung round, pointing up stream and down stream alternatively with the ebb and flow of the tide.

When she arrived she had on board as passengers Captain Baldwin Wake, R.N., and his wife and family. Captain Wake then received the appointment of First Captain Superintendent. Three boys were brought with the ship, too.

I well remember those early days on board, when the mid-stream anchorage tried our patience and endurance badly. In a high wind the ship rolled heavily, making those on board very uncomfortable; and in a big storm it was far from a picnic. We had five years of it, too.

The Mars was now in place, anchored in the Tay, and as the crowds on both sides of the river marvelled at the sight they might have discussed the other major talking point of the day, the building

Figure 3 This, I believe, is the earliest image of the boys, crew and friends aboard the Mars. Captain Scott, third from right, top row, overlooks 118 of his charges. *(Fife Council Libraries and Museums)*

of the Tay Railway Bridge. This was currently causing much controversy in the press, being described in one letter as *about as absurd as a railway to the moon*. The boys and crew of the Mars were to watch the bridge grow slowly, day by day, and be eye-witness to its tragic fall.

The layout of the ship at this time is described in an article from the Lamb Collection:

With a fine figurehead representing the old heathen God of War – Mars – black painted hull and white ports, and smart frigate rigging, she has a fine appearance in the water; and while serving the very important end for which she is designed, she will also form an ornament to the river, and an attraction to the town . . .

Though the Mars has two gun decks, she has four decks in all – namely, the upper deck, the main deck, the lower deck, and the orlop deck. Each of these decks has been cleared of all old and useless material, and is gradually taking the shape which will ultimately be assumed, when the whole fittings have been completed.

. . . Entrance to the ship is obtained by a doorway in the side of the vessel on the lower deck, which is reached by a flight of steps from a strong and well-made platform, a few inches above the water. Passing to the orlop deck the visitor will have presented to his gaze a very spacious compartment, which is to be used as a dormitory. A long row of square wooden pillars runs along the centre, and

from end to end of the ship, and on each side, there will be suspended from the roof, and coming within three feet of the floor, two rows of hammocks with a passage between. By this arrangement the boys will be prevented from inhaling the impure air which may gather near the roof, and be readily observed by the officer as he goes along fulfilling the duties of his watch. In addition to the air holes which originally existed, the ventilation has been increased by a number of windows being made – four on one side and five on the other . . . At the stern there is a department which will be found of interest, to which access is gained by a narrow doorway. Within are two cells, erected for the punishment of any of the boys who may be so unfortunate as to be sent to them, and also a range of 'lockers' for containing in bags any spare clothes – each twelve boys having a locker. In the orlop deck are the entrances to the lower hold, which contains several tanks and the magazines. The tanks have been converted into reservoirs for the reception of rain water, collected from the upper deck by pipes . . .

Emerging from the orlop deck the visitor reaches the lower deck, where the boys will receive their meals, receive their education, and carry on work during winter. About the middle of this deck is a superior hot water heating apparatus, erected by Messrs G. H. & G. Nicoll, and the pipes have been so arranged that in winter clothes may be dried by it. Two pump fire engines are also situated on this deck, and hose communicated from these to every part of the ship. Next the stern a large space is divided off. A room is situated in the centre, and on two sides of it there are three cabins; and on another side a store for boots and the musical instruments.

That above the lower deck is the main deck, where the boys will muster, and where divine service will be held on Sunday and on week days. The fore part of this deck is occupied with a variety of rooms. There is first the cooking galley, with a huge cooking apparatus by Messrs Benham & Sons of London. A fresh water tank is situated in the roof, so that water can be obtained in an instant without leaving the galley, and a 'lift' is situated in one part of the room, by which the boys' meals will be lowered to the mess deck. Next there is a spacious bathroom and lavatory, adequately supplied from tanks with both hot and cold water. Nothing could be better furnished than this place, and its whole arrangement is very skilfully executed. Opposite the cooking galley is the cook's bedroom and storeroom. In another passage, on the other side, are entrances to the lamp-room, the tailor's store-room and workshop, and the hospital with dispensary. The main deck is no less spacious than the others, and it is also well arranged . . . A large drinking tank is situated in the centre. At the aft part the old ward room has been converted into cabins and berths, and there are also the general store room and the kitchen connected with the captain's cabin. Outside the entrance to these rooms a

'rack' has been erected for accommodating the books belonging to the boys. The portholes on all the decks are fitted with plate-glass windows on the folding principle, which secures excellent ventilation.

The spacious upper deck is cleared of everything save the masts, and is set apart for exercise and instruction. An addition has been made to the front of the poop, with the view of cutting off the wind and making the captain's apartments more comfortable. The addition forms a sort of ante-room, about the centre of which is the steering wheel, and at the end an office for the keeping of returns and the transaction of other business. Eight apartments have been set aside for the accommodation of Captain Baldwin Wake, R.N., and have been finely finished. From his rooms access is obtained to the stern gallery, a platform which goes round the stern of the vessel, and forms an excellent promenade. All the hatchways are covered in, and the carpenter's workshop is amidships.

. . . In case of any one falling overboard lifebuoys have been provided, and a chain has been put round the vessel an inch or two above the waterline. She also possesses five boats – a pinnace, two cutters, a gig and a dingy [sic]*.*

We cannot omit to mention an act of very great liberality on the part of Mr Stewart of St Fort. That gentleman has not only granted the privilege of landing and embarking at Woodhaven Pier, but has also by means of pipes brought water from his property for the use of the Mars down to the quay at his own expense.

The amount of work found to be necessary in getting the Mars into order has been enormous, but a better idea of its extent may be formed when we mention that about eighty workmen have been constantly employed on board for several weeks. The Committee have found that their existing funds will be greatly drained away in meeting the expenses which have already been incurred, and we were sure that any appeal which may be made to the community to show their sympathy with them in the shape of a bank note or gold, in such an honourable and noble cause, will not be made in vain.

We understand that the day on which the Mars will be opened as a training ship will be soon fixed, and arrangements made for the inaugural ceremony. The public will afterwards be admitted to inspect the vessel, but the arrangements to enable them to do so will be advertised.

The official opening of the Mars Training Ship Institution was held on board on 20 October 1869, in the presence of a large assemblage of ladies and gentlemen from the neighbouring town of Dundee and the counties of Forfar, Fife and Perth.

Special invitations had been issued, and shortly after noon the Fifeshire left the Craig Pier with the company who had assembled on the Dundee side, while the Atlas brought visitors from the Fife shore.

The day was exceedingly favourable. The sun shone out brilliantly, and the air was not nearly as keen and cold as on the previous day, so that the outing on the river was enjoyed by all. It had been arranged that the ceremonial should take place on the upper deck; and the company, to the number of over a thousand, having all assembled there, Provost Yeaman was called upon to preside.

At the meeting Sir Robert Anstruther addressed the assembly.

We lived in days when economy was a fashionable word, and many people who did not practise it, preached it; but Her Majesty's Government, as they were all aware, were deeply pledged to economy, and they had been very successful in reducing their preaching to practice. But he would venture to suggest that no economy could be so great as a liberal expenditure of money in the prevention of crime. We might imagine that because we allowed only one training ship instead of two that we were saving money. [This may have been a reference to Edinburgh's attempt to get a training ship for the Forth, which had been turned down.] *But the money that we required to expend to keep one*

Figure 4 Interior of the Mars, showing washing troughs, and at the far end, on the left and right, tables set for meal time.
(Dundee City Council Central Library)

criminal would keep six boys, and not only keep six boys, but produce six honest hard-working men instead of one bad man. Where was the economy in refusing a ship, or in cutting down allowances, and allowing the boy to grow up and get into evil ways, and after that his country would have to keep him fifteen or twenty-five years as a convict? It was manifest that the economy was in spending the money early, so as to prevent the boy from falling into bad ways . . .

But it was a fact that the Government allowances per head per week in reformatory establishments was 6/-, whereas the allowance per head per week in industrial establishments was only 4/6. Now, it was very curious why a boy, because he had been put into the reformatory ship for stealing a hen, should be allowed 1/6 more by the Government than they allowed for a boy who was put on the Mars who had never stolen a hen. (Laughter.)

He then comments on the management of the ship:

He had not been a sailor himself, but he had had a good deal to do with soldiers. Now, sailors and soldiers were very much alike, and they were both very like children. He knew something about the management of soldiers, and he knew this, that if a man won their hearts, he could turn them round his thumb; whereas, let a man once, by ignorance or folly, or harshness, set their hearts against him, it would take him years before he could acquire real moral

influence over the men he commanded. (Hear, hear.) If that was true of men, it was a hundred times more true of boys; for, as they knew, their affections were deeper and much more easily aroused. Once secure the hearts of boys who came into the ship, and the superintendent would only have to lift his finger not only to make the boys bow down to him; but to do everything in their power to render him happy, or to confer credit upon the Mars. (Cheers.)

The ship was now almost ready to receive its youthful charges. The Act by which most boys would be admitted to the ship was Clause 14 of the Industrial Schools Act, which asserts:

Any person may bring before Two Justices or a Magistrate any Child apparently under the Age of Fourteen Years that comes within any of the following descriptions, namely:–

That is found begging or receiving Alms (whether actually or under the pretext of selling or offering for Sale any Thing), or being in any Street or public Place for the purpose of so begging or receiving Alms.

That is found wandering and not having any Home or settled place of Abode, or proper Guardianship, or visible means of Subsistence.

That is found destitute, either being an Orphan or having a surviving Parent who is undergoing Penal Servitude or Imprisonment.

That frequents the company of reputed Thieves.

The Justices or Magistrates before whom a

Child is brought as coming within One of these Descriptions, if satisfied on Inquiry of that fact, and that it is expedient to deal with him under this Act, may order him to be sent to a certified Industrial School.

Each boy, when presented to the ship, would be given a ship number, by which he would be known from that time onwards. The boy with the first number 1 was Dundonian David Petrie, who was registered on board on 22 October 1869, yet he was not the first boy to be admitted. That 'honour' goes to the boy (ship number 15) Murdoch McLeod. Murdoch, originally from Logiealmond, was also the first voluntary boy – that is, a boy who joined the ship by his own choice – and was registered on board on 13 October. In an interview he gave in Dundee in 1939, he recounts his story:

'At 13 I was apprenticed to a firm of bookbinders in Perth,' he said. 'The firm got the job of rebinding books which were damaged in a fire at Perth Library. Flicking the pages of one book, I found it was about the adventures of "Swiss Family Robinson". The foreman allowed me to take it home on pain of skelping if I did not return it the next day.

'I read the book. "This", I said to myself, "would be the life – no musty work-shop for me." So that night I decided to run away to sea.'

He described how he had commandeered a boat in Perth, rowed down the Tay on the ebb tide, and had come ashore in the carse.

He supped that night on strawberries from a field, suffered for his over-indulgence; slept the night in a hay stack, and walked into Dundee.

A STOWAWAY

Creeping on board a brig about to sail for Archangel, he hid among coils of rope in the fo'castle, but was detected by a sailor, who hauled him before the captain.

'I wish to become a sailor, sir,' he said.

'Well, there is a man-o-war just in from Sheerness, and they are looking for boys like you,' the captain replied, referring to an old line-of-battleship, H.M.S. Mars, which was to be used as a training ship. A policeman took Murdoch to the man-o-war which he joined voluntarily as a trainee, No.1 boy on the Mars . . .

It is a fascinating insight into how one boy ended up on the Mars, and we shall come upon Murdoch McLeod later in the book. In the Blyth Hall, in Newport-on-Tay, the Admission and Discharge books list every boy who stood upon the Mars. The first ten boys are as follows.

No. 1 David Petrie, thirteen years old, was admitted on 22 October 1869, was charged under Section 14 with being *Destitute and Homeless* and sentenced to three years on board. His parents are *James and Sarah Petrie*, his father is *a seaman, whereabouts unknown*, and his mother's address is given as *Dron's Close, Dundee*. David's character is given as *indifferent* and his religion is *Protestant*. Normally there is a physical description of each boy but none in his

We'll Send Ye Tae the Mars

case, and like so many Mars boys he could neither write, read, nor calculate. (The book used to test the boys' reading ability was Nelson's No. 1 Junior Reader.) The page also contains a section to mark their progress while on board; the only comment in his case is *good*. The notes on his discharge read, *Discharged, 28th of January 1871, apprenticed to Stephen and Son, ship owners, Dundee liner 'Arctic', whaler*.

No. 2 George Boon, thirteen years old, admitted on 22 October, was charged under Section 14 with *Destitution* and sentenced to three years' detention. His parents are *Martha Boon*, whose address is given as *London*, and his father is dead. George's previous character is given as *idle wanderer* and his religion is *Protestant*. He is described as *4ft 7 and a quarter*, his figure is described as *stout* (which undoubtedly means strong or sturdy, as in 'stout-hearted men', as it's unlikely that many of these poor wee souls would be chubby). He has a *swarthy complexion, light hair, grey eyes* with a *strait nose* [sic]. It is noted that *he cannot read, write or calculate* and his mental capacity is described as *slow*. Marks on person and other peculiarities: *number 2 on left arm*. He also had a *bracelet on his right wrist and 'SB' on the back of right hand*. His progress is noted in 1871 as *1st class for conduct, intelligence and industry*. Later they describe him as *a quiet, steady, good boy*.

No. 3 William Alexander, thirteen years old. Was admitted on 22 October and charged under Section 14 with *Wandering Destitute*, and sentenced to three years' detention. His parents are *William and Mary Alexander*, whose address is given as *Candle Lane Close, Dundee*. William's character is described as *worthless*, which seems unkind, at best, as his parental situation is described as *father dead*

and abandoned by his mother. Marks on person: *No. 3 on right arm and an anchor on his right hand*. He is described as *4ft 8in with red hair, hazel eyes and can read but not write*.

No. 4 Thomas Bell, aged fourteen, admitted on 22 October, was charged under Section 14 with being a *Homeless Wanderer* and detained for two years. His previous character is described as *wandering in idleness, his father is dead and his mother, Jane Bell, lives in Mid Wynd, Hawkhill, Dundee*. His character is given as *in destitution, he can read a little but cannot write or calculate*. In December 1870 his conduct and character entry is *1st class for conduct*. He is *discharged in December 1870 to the Royal Navy* but is found to be *invalided for defective vision and joined the Merchant Service*.

No. 5 Thomas Purgavie, aged twelve years, admitted under Section 14 for *wandering neglected* and sentenced to four years' detention; previous character is *vagrant*. His father is *William Purgavie his whereabouts are unknown*, and his mother, *Isabella Blair, lives at Lochee by Dundee*. His character is described as *destitute, he reads a little* and his conduct in March 1871 is described as *good*. Yet on 10 March 1871 he is *transferred to an Industrial School, boy subject to fits*.

No. 6 Patrick Foy, aged thirteen, was admitted on 22 October under Section 14 and charged with being an *idle wanderer*. *Owen Foy, the boy's father, is dead*, and his mother, *Mary Foy, sews sacks for employment, she lives in Dens Road, Dundee*. His religion is given as *Roman Catholic* and his character on 1 April 1871 is given *as 1st class for conduct, a steady, well behaved boy. 30th September, 1st class for conduct steady intelligent and exemplary boy*. His height is *4ft 10 and a quarter, figure stout, complexion dark, hair dark with* hazel eyes and a flat nose. *Marks on person, a 'P' on right arm and a blue 'D' on back of right hand with a scar on his forehead. His health is good* but he has *no education and his mental capacity is slow.*

No. 7 James Graham, aged thirteen years, was admitted on 22 October, charged under Section 14 and sentenced for three years for being a *homeless wanderer.* His mother is unknown and his *father, Robert Graham, a slater from Haddington, has abandoned the boy.* His character is described as *worthless. His height is 4ft 10in, his figure is stout, and he has a swarthy complexion, brown hair and his eyes are grey and small.* Marks on his person: *a thistle on the upper part of his left arm, very little eyelashes, his health is good and though he reads a little, cannot write or calculate and his mental capacity is slow.* His conduct on 1 April 1871 is *1st class, boy quiet and responding, usually well behaved but untidy in person. 30th September 1871, 1st class for conduct, but much improved, is more cheerful and is very well behaved.*

No. 8 David Macfarlane, aged twelve, was admitted on 22 October and sentenced at Dundee Sheriff Court under Section 14 and sentenced to four years on the Mars. His previous character is described as *uncontrolled and neglected,* and his parents *David and Mary Macfarlane are from Dundee. His height is 4ft 8in and his figure is stout with fair complexion, brown hair and hazel eyes. Marks on person, scar on right cheek, anchor on left arm, figure of a man on inner part of left arm, anchor on back of right hand. He cannot read, write or calculate and his mental capacity is fair.* Conduct and character in school: *1st April 1870, 1st class for conduct, well behaved and clean boy. 30th September 1871, 1st class for conduct a steady good boy. 1st January 1872 +C, 20th June 1872 +C ex.*

No. 9 William McIntosh, aged twelve, was admitted 23 October, and charged with being *destitute and homeless* under Section 14. He is described as being an *idle wanderer.* His parents: *George, his father, is dead and his mother Charlotte McIntosh is alive and her address is given as Annfield Road, Dundee.* William's attitude is described as *indifferent,* and *he can't read, write or calculate.* His progress is noted as being *a good boy.* Tragically, the last comment on his admission page is *was drowned on the 13 of March 1871 at the mouth of the Tay.* More of that story later.

No. 10 Joseph Pitt, aged thirteen, was admitted on 23 October and sentenced at the *Dundee Burgh Magistrates* under Section 14 as a *homeless orphan* to three years' detention. Obviously both parents were dead, and Joseph *reads and writes a little.* He is discharged from the Mars on the *18th July 1870, employment found for boy by Captain Wake R.N.*

By December 1869, there had been 102 boys admitted to the Mars. Even though the Committee had spent £3,000 on the ship, fitting up and painting her, it would still have felt uncomfortably exposed, and the swivel anchor must have made it a rocky experience. The weather, that first winter on board, was bitterly cold, as fields of ice came down the Tay:

> *On the south side, and towards low water, the Mars Training Ship was more than once surrounded and she appeared like a vessel in the Arctic regions. The ice yesterday was of no great thickness, but if the frost continues it will rapidly increase in depth, and it will be necessary to have the bows of the Mars protected at the water line. Communication with the Fife shore will also become difficult, and it will be well to have*

abundant supplies on board. Captain Wake came over to Dundee yesterday to make all the needful arrangements.

The relevance of this report is brought into sharp focus when we read of an incident which occurred on 23 December, involving Captain Wake yet again saving a life (boy no. 6, Patrick Foy) in these freezing conditions:

A gallant deed was performed by Captain Wake, R.N., of Her Majesty's ship Mars, yesterday when one of the boys, on coming out of a boat, missed his footing and fell overboard. It was but the work of a minute to reach the poop and heave the life buoy towards him, which was done with great precision, lighting within a yard of the drowning lad, but by this time he was much too excited and exhausted to take hold of it as it came to his reach. Captain Wake no sooner received this from the stern-walk where he was standing, than he stripped himself of his coat, and did not hesitate in taking a leap of some 26 feet, reaching the boy just in time to save him from a watery grave. The conduct of the gallant Captain showed how much he has the welfare of the boys at heart, and the dangers that he will brave for their sakes.

The Dundee Humane Society presented Captain Wake with a parchment, as a mark of the public appreciation of his courage and magnanimity:

The Dundee Humane Society hereby record their high approbation of the gallant conduct of Captain Baldwin Arden Wake on the 23rd December 1869, [who] leaped overboard to the rescue of one of the boys, and saved him from drowning, in the southern waters of the Tay. By this parchment the Dundee Humane Society, as a committee of the public, desire to express, in a lasting form, the universal praise which Captain Wake's generous daring, in plunging overboard from a height of twenty six feet to the rescue of a fellow creature, has worthily elicited.

It is difficult to imagine why the brave captain should have been removed after yet another addition to his list of deeds of gallantry. Yet, after a visit to the ship, the report of Her Majesty's Inspector of Reformatory and Industrial Schools, the Reverend Sydney Turner, cast doubt on Captain Wake's methods:

The Mars training ship was inspected on the 21st September and also the 21st of December . . . The admissions have been too rapid, and the Inspector on his visit in December doubted whether the system of management by Captain Wake was likely to be successful.

No other reasons have come to light for Captain Wake's dismissal. By May 1870 he had left the ship. It may be that, at the age of fifty-six, this was not a suitable position for him; he may or may not have been a disciplinarian — but there was a strange event which

Figure 5 Alexander McDougall, the ship's carpenter, putting a few of the boys through their paces.   *(Dundee City Council Central Library)*

happened in 1866. The Centre for Whistler Studies website describes how, while he was working as a mail agent on the *Shannon*, en route from Valparaiso to Britain, he was in a brawl with James McNeill Whistler (the American artist). Apparently they had fallen out after certain disparaging remarks were made with reference to Mr Whistler's having to share his table with a negro. Wake and Whistler came to blows, and on the following day, there was a knock on James Whistler's cabin door. Mr Whistler takes up the tale:

The morning after the negro affair was Sunday – and we were to reach Southampton that afternoon – Captain Wake in full uniform came to my cabin – I received him with cold politeness, imagining that he came to apologize for the insulting language used towards me, on the previous day, by him alone among those on board, he [Captain Wake] being a strong abolitionist.

I had refused to notice this at the time, as I told him, because of the difference in our ages – Judge then of his conduct:– He served me with a long and impertinent sermon, in which Providence and the Negro race played equal parts, the whole thing being of a Sabbath Baptist Meeting tone! After listening patiently, at his request, to it all, I said, This is all very well, but not to the purpose! I supposed that you came to apologize for your ungentlemanly language to me yesterday. Hereupon my preacher changed his style, and forgetful of peaceful missions, loudly proclaimed that it was perfectly true that he had insulted me, and had done so deliberately! – and

wished it to be understood that he then did so again! – Moreover that nothing but cowardice on my part would have prevented me before or could now prevent me from resenting it! . . .

Whereupon unable to stand these repeated outrages I slapped his face with my left hand, my right being utterly maimed and disabled since the day before! – I being forced to wear it in a sling – a fact patent throughout the whole saloon – and which probably brought the valiant . . . Captain to the charge!

He thereupon rushed at me and beating down easily my disabled arm, struck me a violent blow in my eye with what must have been a ring on his finger. The Marine Guard immediately sprang in and hauled him off – when two Gentlemen who were present at the whole affair, came up to express their loud indignation at this foolish and outrageous conduct – This indignation and disgust was so thoroughly participated in by the officers and gentlemen on board, that they showed it openly at the dinner table; and Dr Crosbie, a naval officer returning from Jamaica, went to the Captain of the Ship and stated distinctly that Capt Wake had by his proceedings, disgraced the cloth he wore.

We can only imagine that this episode was not mentioned at the interview for the position of Captain Superintendent of the Mars. A certain intolerance of others' opinions (no matter how unpleasant those opinions might be), mixed with extreme volatility, may not have been desirable attributes for his future role. In the Mars minute books dated 5 February 1874 a letter from Captain Wake is read to the Committee:

> *There was a memorial from Captain Wake; late Captain Superintendent of the Mars representing the pecuniary difficulties under which he presently is; and that as these difficulties were brought about by his being unexpectedly discharged from the Mars, making a claim for compensation against this Institution. The secretary was instructed to write to Captain Wake in reply, and to state that the Committee did not think he had ground of claim against the Institution. And to express the regret of the Committee at his making a request with which they could not comply.*

Captain Wake's death was no less extraordinary than his life had been:

> *On 16th January 1880, Wake left Nanaimo Harbour in his small sloop, planning to sail to his settler homestead on Valdez Island [near Anchorage in Alaska]. He never arrived . . . His son, George Wake, offered a reward for information leading to any clues about the disappearance of his father. Wake's body was never found.*

Headlines from Dundee newspapers in 1870

February: Alleged Plot to Assassinate Emperor Napoleon

April: The Sioux Indians are reported to be resuming hostilities, and there are said to be 20,000 of them on the 'war path'.

May: Republican Riots in Paris

June: Death of Charles Dickens (He had appeared at the New Public Halls, Dundee, on Friday 1 and Saturday 2 October 1858, reading from his works, including *A Christmas Carol*.)

3

Captain Charles Casely Scott

With the unceremonious removal of Captain Wake, on Thursday, 28 April 1870, a successor was appointed as Captain Superintendent of the Mars. The newspapers announced that *the difficulties between Captain Wake and the Directors have been arranged, and Captain Scott has now been engaged as chief officer, the staff consists of six seamen instructors, including cook and carpenter.*

Captain Scott had been the First Officer on the ship under Captain Wake, and therefore a natural successor and, at forty-four years old, he possibly had a less dogmatic view of his role than Captain Wake. From the *Piper O' Dundee* we read:

Staff Commander Captain Charles Casely Scott appears to have joined the Royal Navy at the age of 14 and from the Royal Navy we learn that he served continuously in all parts of the world up to the time of his being appointed to the Mars. As navigating Midshipman of H.M.S. Alert he was in 1844 employed off the West coast of Africa in the suppression of the slave trade, and was engaged in the attack on a Moorish fort. In 1850, whilst serving in the H.M.S.

Daedalus as acting Navigating Lieutenant, he was wounded whilst in command of the boats of that vessel destroying the villages of a hostile tribe at Vancouver's Island.

Captain Scott took part in the famous search expedition in the arctic regions for Sir John Franklin. He has served on the China, Mediterranean, Brazil and Pacific stations and was one of the officers selected by the Admiralty for special services in the Baltic at the commencement of the Russian War . . .

It would appear that although most of the officers on the Mars were English, and Captain Scott was born *South of the Tweed*, his Scottish ancestry, and the fact that for some years he had served on the Guard Ship at South Queensferry, made it easier for him to relate to and converse with his Scottish charges. Nevertheless, there can be little doubt that this would be no easy task for the Captain; these were uncharted waters, and the famous naval tradition of turning a blind eye would not go far here. There was a public face to wear, the reputation of the institution to uphold, punishment books to keep, minuted monthly meetings to hold and regular government inspections to undergo, plus the discipline of up to 400 boys to maintain, without 'rocking the boat'.

On 3 May the Mars Committee ran into a storm, which may have made some of them think twice about their involvement in the Mars Institution. It happened at a meeting of the Commission of Supply at the County Hall, Cupar, when Captain Maitland Dougall, as chairman of the Prison Board (and a member of the General Committee of the Mars), was attempting to extricate an extra £50 from the Commission.

Figure 6 Captain Charles Casely Scott, RN, Captain Superintendent 1870–92.
(Fife Council Libraries and Museums)

Captain Maitland Dougall is recorded as saying:

It might be in the remembrance of those present that when last year it was proposed to start an industrial training school, to make young sailors, the County was kind enough to grant, as the Counties of Forfar and Perth did also each grant, a sum of £200 for an industrial training school. As it was thought at that time there would also be a training ship on the Forth, the sum Fife granted was divided into two – £100 was given to the Tay Committee, and £100 was kept in reserve for the Forth ship; but it had been found that Government was unwilling to grant a second ship in the eastern district of Scotland until it should be found that one ship was insufficient . . .

His reason for doing this was that with the expense of the officers on the ship, and with the same amount of caulking and keeping up of the ship as had been required, it would be found that, while she was only half full of boys the funds would be insufficient . . .

Mr Wemyss, in replying to Captain Maitland Dougall, also directed his comments towards Captain Ogilvy Dalgleish, another Mars Committee member; they were both to find out that charity and friendship seldom go hand in hand.

Mr Wemyss of Wemyss Hall contested – The County was not sufficiently represented at the board of the training ship, considering that they were called upon to subscribe. They should know not only how their money was applied, but how business in general was carried on. He would particularly allude to something that had taken place just now – the notified dismissal of the present Captain and Superintendent [Captain Wake] almost without, he believed, reasons given. He thought that was not fair treatment, and that even the Admiralty, arbitrary as they were, would never dismiss a captain from his post without making charges against him, and endeavouring to prove that he was inefficient. So far as he could make out from what he had seen, he thought he was a man very well adapted for his office. He judged from the capital order these boys were in, and from the very great advance they had made for the very short time they had been in the ship, that Captain Wake was a fit man for the post. He proved himself to be a brave and humane man, by leaping into the water to save the life of one of the boys. (Hear, hear.) That he was a kind man, he [Major Wemyss] knew from the conduct of the boys when they were told he was going away from them. The information was met by them with a general burst of sobs and tears – they were so fond of him. The sending him away was ruining his character as an officer. He might never get employment again; and he believed it was ruining him in circumstances to a considerable extent, and from the great expense he would be put to by the change. Such an arbitrary dismissal of the Captain he thought was improper.

Such a comprehensive attack on the management of the ship by Major Wemyss must have come as quite a shock to the well-meaning members of the Mars General Committee, who were unlikely to have been talked to before in such a manner and so publicly. Captain Ogilvy Dalgleish replied:

He was sorry that his friend Major Wemyss had gone into a matter which ought not to have come up there. He had spoken of a Captain of the Navy dismissed in an arbitrary way; but Captain Wake had held his appointment not as naval officer, but as an individual appointed by the Tay Committee – elected to take charge of this training school. He was engaged for a limited period. His services were engaged for one year. During that year it had been the business of the Committee, almost every one of them, to support him and to do what they could for the good of the Institution. But that appointment expires in June, and it came to be a question whether they should enter into a new engagement with Captain Wake or not, and it was resolved that they should not do so. He [Captain Dalgleish] did not know how that could involve the character of Captain Wake in the least degree. All they say is that they do not reappoint him. Captain Dalgleish concluded by saying that, as a member of the Committee, he had endeavoured to do his duty, but, if it was the wish of subscribers to have a new Committee, he would be happy to retire.

Dr Watson Wemyss thought the much more proper and more handsome way to subscribe the £50 would be just to state that in consequence of the favourable report they had heard from the members of the Committee they had much pleasure in handing [over] the increased donation.

A storm in a teacup, or a shot across the bows for the management Committee of the Mars from those who held the purse strings? It may have been the first skirmish, but it would certainly not be the last!

The admission of boys on board the Mars continued, and a steady procession of boys filled the empty spaces from all over the country. Of the 229 admitted up to December 1871, 165 boys came through the court in Dundee, and the rest from Fife, Perth and Forfarshire. There was the odd one from Portobello or Galashiels, and the home address of John Ireland, who came up with the ship from Sheerness, is given as City Road, London. Although the Mars was the only training ship to admit Roman Catholic boys in Scotland, out of the number admitted so far there were only 55 Roman Catholics but 228 Protestants on board, and one with no religious persuasion. This was to change dramatically when the influx from Glasgow and Edinburgh began.

From a small pamphlet reprinted from the *Dundee Advertiser* of 1870, we get a fascinating glimpse of early life on board:

A DAY AND NIGHT ON THE MARS TRAINING SHIP

The discipline followed on board the Mars is based on that existing in the Royal Navy. The Mars is commanded by Staff-Commander C. Scott, R.N., an officer of standing and reputation. Under him are the boatswain, master-at-arms, two seamen instructors, one carpenter, and one cook. Mr Brydie, the

schoolmaster, has charge of the educational branch of instruction.

As we pass the entering-port, we find conspicuously before us the following printed regulations for the guidance of the officers and boys:–

1.– Remember that God's eye is always on us.

2.– Never take His Holy Name in vain.

3.– Never tell a lie, even at the risk of punishment, nor use bad language.

4.– Never steal, never fight, strike, or quarrel.

5.– Never do anything your conscience tells you is wrong.

6.– Keep the Sabbath-day holy.

7.– Keep yourself clean, and be careful of your clothes.

8.– Do not spit about the decks, or go on the upper deck without your cap.

9.– Do not lounge about the entering port, or put your head out of any of the ports.

10.– Do not hang your clothes or towels on the hot water pipes, or in any other place but that appointed.

11.– Move about smartly but quietly. All shouting at each other, talking, skylarking on duty, and in your hammocks, is strictly forbidden.

12.– It is strictly forbidden to call to any one passing the ship in a boat, or to make signs to them.

13.– It will be considered as great an offence to disobey the orders of a petty officer as to disobey the captain or other officers of the ship.

14.– No cards, dice, or gambling of any sort to be allowed in any part of the ship.

Boys will understand that by strictly attending to the above rules they will add to their own comfort; manifest a desire to do well; and will always be rewarded. No boy who does his best, or, on committing a fault, at once acknowledges it, and promises amendment, need fear punishment. It will be the captain's study to make all on board happy; and he will expect the boys to deserve encouragement by observing all the regulations of the ship, and show a cheerful spirit in the performance of their duties.

Chas C. Scott, Captain Superintendent,
Industrial Training Ship Mars, 29th June 1870.

. . . The boys [200 on board at this time] are particularly under the charge of the officers – the first 40 on the list being under the Boatswain, Nos. 41 to 90 are under the master-at-arms, 91 to 140 under the 1st Instructor, 141 upwards under the 2nd Instructor. The officers are responsible for their own

Figure 7 The Mars boys hard at work in the schoolroom.
(*Dundee Art Galleries and Museums*)

divisions as to cleanliness, condition of their clothes, and attention to the duties prescribed by the routine; they are directed to teach them habits of order and regularity, to encourage feelings of emulation and cheerfulness; they are to bear in mind that many of the boys will err from ignorance of their new life; they are to act with kindness and firmness, never relaxing strict discipline, but encouraging a system of rewards rather than of punishment. These instructions are copied almost verbatim from the written orders of Captain Scott, indicating the beneficial influence flowing from the fountain head.

These are fine words, but they are only that. How the ship is managed depends on strong leadership; the question is, will Captain Scott rise to the challenge? We are now guided through the daily routine by the same correspondent.

We have left orders with the officer of the watch to be called at 4.45 a.m., and punctually to the minute he comes. On the maindeck we meet Captain Scott already looking on. The bell strikes two – it is 5 a.m. – and at once the boatswain's pipe is heard, and his stentorian voice shouts, 'Hands turn out.' In a single instant, from perfect stillness, the orlop deck is alive. Within five minutes each boy is dressed and standing in line at the head of his hammock. At 5.05 a.m. the bell is tolled for prayer, as it is also before the usual morning and evening services, and has a very fine and solemnising effect. The boatswain calls for the first two verses of the 'Morning Hymn';

the young, fresh voices take it up, sing it well, and he must be made of sterner stuff than we are who could listen to the beautiful words under such circumstances without a tear coming to the heart's relief. The verses sung, the boys face inwards, and pass a minute or two in silent prayer; then comes the boatswain with his pipe, and 'Lash up and stow hammocks' is the command.

. . . The morning is wet, and the hammocks are stowed on the orlop deck, in divisions and according to numbers, so that no confusion occurs when they are required at night. At 5.25 again we hear the 'shrill whistle', and 'Wash decks' is the command. We pass our time in writing during a part of the hour and twenty minutes which are thus occupied, and as we write we hear the shrieking whistles of the Dundee factories proclaiming that the labours of the day are not yet there begun.

. . . At 6.30 the jolly boat boys are called away. They are off to Woodhaven for milk for breakfast. At 6.45 the cooks of the messes go to the galley for the porridge, and put out the basins and divide the milk. At 6.50 the drum beats, and all hands fall in on the main deck. They are ranged in line in messes under the respective captains of the messes, who see that they are all present, the master-at-arms ensuring attendance by looking round the decks with a suspicious-looking cane in his hands. The bell strikes six – it is 7 a.m., and at once the boys scamper down

to the lower deck, range themselves at their respective mess tables, when the following grace is very beautifully sung, as it is before every meal, all present uncovered:–

'Be present at our table, Lord,

Be here and everywhere adored;

Thy creatures bless, and grant that we

In Paradise may dwell with Thee.'

The breakfast is plentiful, the porridge well boiled, the milk good (we ourselves breakfasted on the same), and it is eaten with zeal which would excite the envy of many a poor dyspeptic, who exists in some of our many miserable, ill-aired closes and wynds. At 8 comes the leading formality of the morning. The band musters on the poop, playing 'God save the Queen', and the ensign floats from the peak.

At 7.30 the boys wash and dress, and clean up the lower deck. They put their bags containing their spare clothes in order, and at 8.15 the pipe calls attention, and 'Stow bags' is the order. They are stowed in divisions in what was the bread-room, in the after part of the orlop deck. At 8.30 all hands fall in, previous to divisions, with their towels in their hands, for inspection by the respective officers of divisions – their trousers rolled up above their knees, and shirt sleeves above their elbows.

At 8.40 the towels are stopped on to the clothes line and hoisted up to dry. At 8.50 the drum beats, and

there are divisions, the principal inspection of the day, when the Captain, accompanied by the boatswain, inspects each boy as he passes around the deck.

At 9 a.m. there was divine service, *simple and appropriate – just such a service as we find in the worship of a private family.*

At 9.15 one watch goes to school, where they are taught reading, writing, and arithmetic. The other watch are then told off to their different duties by the boatswain, who from his slate calls out the numbers of the boys wanted for a particular service; they fall-in in squads as they are called, and then march off, some to exercising reefing and furling the topsail, some to duty in boats, some to knotting and splicing, others to painting, or other necessary duties. A few boys are always employed assisting the tailor, a few under the carpenter; while others take it in turns to act as officers' servants . . . The watch at school one day is at practical training the next. On Wednesday and Saturday afternoons the boys are landed for recreation and amusement . . .

At 12.30 the order is given to 'Clear up decks.' Work ceases, the school is dismissed. At 12.45 the cooks of the messes go to the galley and prepare for dinner; at 12.50 the successive rolls of the drum call all hands to fall in; and as two bells strike, being one p.m., they go to dinner as they did to breakfast, singing the grace before beginning . . .

From 1.30, when dinner is finished, there is three-quarters of an hour for recreation and sky-

larking. At 2.15 again one watch goes to school, the other to their respective practical labours. At 5 p.m. the pipe stops the labour and dismisses the school . . .

> *5.30 supper of tea, milk and biscuits is served . . . and at 6 it is time for recreation; in fine weather a party leaves to bathe, others play marbles on deck. There are also ninepins, fencing foils, and draughts, while some read.*

By 9 o'clock it's time for prayers and by 9.30 all boys are in their hammocks.

This excellent piece gives a snapshot of life on board the Mars. It seems a long day, and there is every chance that by the time the boys reached their hammocks, they would be too exhausted for 'skylarking'. Interestingly, while the writer was on board, a new arrival was admitted to the ship:

> *He is twelve years of age, was deserted ten years ago by his father, has a mother who works at a mill and neglects him; he has been ill fed, is in rags, can neither read nor write, and presents a striking contrast to his shipmates. He disappears for an hour, and is then seen amongst the others, his hair cut, his person thoroughly cleaned in the bath. He is clothed in the ship's uniform, and is surrounded by a group of the initiated, who are following him about the ship.*

Figure 8 This magnificent photograph of the Mars Training Ship, taken from Woodhaven, shows what an impressive sight she was, seen from either side of the river, or from the Tay Railway Bridge.
(Dundee City Council Central Library)

> *Next morning as we leave the ship we find him crying bitterly. Bad as his home has been, it is still home. He looks wistfully at the shore, which he cannot reach; but a few days will cure all this, and render him as happy and comfortable as the others.*

What is not mentioned here is that the boys, on admission, are given a ship number and that this was applied to their uniform, toothbrush and other belongings. From that moment on, they would cease to be called by their own name, but always addressed by their number, even by their shipmates. A Mr G. K. Goalen, who saw the boys playing in Elie, recalls in a letter printed in the *Dundee Courier*:

> *They didn't know each other by name – only by number. Then, when at football on the turf, they would shout come oan 'twa-sna-twa' (272), or 'twa-erry-seeven' (287) &c.*

The registration and numbering system had to be adapted, as the number of boys passing through the ship increased. Eventually, when the registration number reached 619, they decided to number the boys on a rotation of 400; James Lawson, from Dunshalt, became ship number 13 and his registration number was 619. This was to save renumbering articles such as hammocks and uniforms when they were reused.

The Mars was now establishing itself and becoming a focus of great attention on the Tay, for those both on land and on the often congested river and busy port. It is hard to imagine the amount of traffic on the river at that time. Often there would be fifty to a hundred boats of all shapes and sizes sailing on the Tay, many simply for pleasure. For the boys on board, this must have been a pleasant distraction.

On Saturday, 21 May 1870:

PROCESSION OF BOATS ROUND THE MARS

By way of notifying in a formal sort of manner that the rowing season on the lower part of the river Tay has now commenced, the members of the Newport Rowing Club had a procession over the waters on Saturday afternoon . . .

Long boats, short boats, and boats which like Sandy Thamson's leg, were neither long nor short, but something 'atween the twa', manned by figures in red, white, blue, pink, and – etcetera coloured uniforms, twisted here and there in the basin, making it for the time being a scene of animated confusion. [A flotilla of thirty-three boats began to parade around the Mars.] *. . . A fleet of 'outsiders' composed of heavy rowing boats, sailing boats, and little steamers, 'waited' on the line, and the occupants of these encouraged the rowers by freely criticising their boats, their uniforms, and themselves. Most of the 'attendants' dropped off at the Mars, which had hoisted a display of bunting in recognition of the Club. The boys on board the big ship had received permission to view the procession as best they could, and when it drew near the little fellows rather astonished the 'landsmen' by rushing up the masts with the swiftness of a flock of squirrels. The fearless youngsters suspended themselves from the ropes and yardarms, and two were balanced apparently with the utmost comfort on the top of the main and mizzen masts. The crews gave them a hearty cheer as the procession passed. Having rounded the Mars, the line turned eastwards, and ran briskly down to the old pier at Newport, where the rowers landed, and adjourned in a body to Mr Dickson's Hall.*

This was possibly the first public recognition that the Mars had arrived, and it was to become a major part of Dundee's social and civic life. For the next sixty years, few events were deemed complete without at least some input from the ship's boys.

An advert was placed in the *Hampshire Telegraph and Sussex Chronicle* on 10 August 1870. (The Mars band would become a crucial part of the ship's life and income.)

Wanted Immediately;

For the Training Ship Mars at Dundee, NB., a master-at-arms, qualified to instruct boys in drum and fife and band bugle. Pay £1 3/- a week, no rations.

Testimonials, statement of age, and if married.

To be sent to Commander C. C. Scott, R.N., Captain Superintendent.

On Wednesday, 21 September 1870, a celebration was held on board, to mark the first anniversary of the opening of the ship, which was attended by over 1,000 guests.

In beautiful weather they gathered on board, the music on this occasion being provided by the 1st Forfarshire Rifle Volunteers who struck up with martial spirit 'Rule Britannia'. This was a chance to see the advances the boys had made in such a short time.

In quick obedience of order the little fellows all of a sudden began to ascend the rigging with remarkable agility, and in a moment's time the yards were 'manned'. The rapidity and order in which the ceremony was gone through elicited admiration and deserved praise.

. . . Lord Dalhousie was the first to ascend the gangway from the steamer to the Mars, and as he did so the band announced his approach by playing 'Laird o' Cockpen'.

Of course, the Mars was not the only training ship in the country; by February 1871 many others were flourishing:

Formidable, Bristol; Havannah, Cardiff; Southampton, Hull; Clarence and Indefatigable, Mersey; Conway and Akbar, Liverpool; Chichester, Kent; Worcester, Southend; Warspite, Woolwich; Cornwall, Purfleet; Cumberland, Glasgow, and lastly the Mars.

Total expenditure to this time [on the Mars] is £3,139 on furnishings; wages, clothing, and provisions, £4,167 10s. 9d.; in all £7,306 10s. 9d. Although the 'Mars' has accommodation for a large number of boys, it is not probable the number will over much exceed 250 at one time. The Committee will encourage them to go into the Royal Navy and

Merchant Service as soon as they are sufficiently trained, which will keep the number down. Besides, the Home Department does not favour a large number being on board one ship. The expenses per head cannot, on the lowest estimate, be stated at less than £20 16/- per annum. The expenses of the boys on board the 'Mars' have as yet considerably exceeded that rate. Eight boys are in course of being transferred to the Royal Navy with consent of the Admiralty.

The weather over the winter had been exceedingly cold: in November of 1870, *the thermometer at Newport stood at 18 degrees, being 14 degrees of frost, the lowest point since 1854.* The cold gave way to stormy conditions, and the weather report mentioned strong gales for Saturday 11 and Sunday 12 March 1871. This was the beginning of a series of events that would shake the Mars Institution to its very foundations. Captain Scott could not have prepared himself for the inquisition that was to follow the tragedy:

FATAL ADVENTURE OF THREE MARS BOYS

Yesterday [Monday, 13 March] *the River Tay was the scene of a melancholy and foolhardy act on the part of three boys, which had terminated fatally in the case of at least one of the lads. About seven o'clock yesterday morning, five boys were sent ashore from the Mars in the 'dingy' [sic] for the letters. On landing at Woodhaven Pier two of them went down to the Fife boat for letters. The three who remained procured an old sail from the shed at the pier, and on the two boys coming down with the letters their comrades tried to persuade them to go to Mr Grant's Inn for a biscuit. This the lads refused to do, and, seeing that the three in the boat were bent on leaving them, one of those on shore seized hold of the boat and held on. One of the occupants of the boat then, it is said, drew his knife, and under threat of being stabbed in the hand the boy withdrew it. Immediately the boat was pushed off and the sail set . . .*

The boat was seen at the ferry pier, and also by those on board the steamer. She was observed to pass Broughty Ferry and Tayport, and the spectators thought it a dangerous thing for three lads to be going out in such a day. In the meantime the two lads informed Constable McCormack of what had happened . . .

He then went across to Broughty Ferry, and telegraphed from the Preventive Station there to Carnoustie, Arbroath, and Buddonness Lighthouse. The reply from the latter place was a query asking if the boat had a sail. On being answered in the affirmative, the lighthouse-keeper telegraphed that he had seen such a boat, and would go up to make her out again. He did so, but could see no trace of the boat; and he sent word that he thought she must have stood out to sea, as it was too rough for any small boat to land.

Captain Scott, being informed of the circumstances, also telegraphed to the places mentioned, and sent men on both sides of the river to ascertain whether any trace could be found of the boat and the adventurers. He went to Carnoustie, but at the time of his being there no appearance of the fugitives could be discovered . . . Captain Edwards of the Star o' Tay . . . was told that a boat belonging to the Mars had passed about nine o'clock. The sail was all torn, and the men on board the cutter told Captain Edwards that the boat was likely to get amongst broken water . . .

About seven o'clock at night a telegram was received in Dundee from the Buddonness Lighthouse stating that the dead body of a boy had been washed ashore on the sands. Further on information was received from the police at Carnoustie intimating that the boat had been driven on shore bottom up, that the oars had been washed ashore, and that the body of a boy, with the number '82' on his uniform, had been cast on the sands. This body awaits identification, but one of the boys' numbers was known to be about '80'. [His actual number was 81.]

THE DROWNING OF THREE MARS BOYS
Finding of Another Body

On Tuesday morning about 6 o'clock, one of the coast guard men, named David Johnston, stationed at Carnoustie, discovered the body floating about six yards from the beach, about 800 yards east of Buddonness lighthouse. He at once brought it ashore, and reported the circumstance to Captain McKinnon, of the Coastguard, who sent a cart for it and had it conveyed to the dead-house, where the body found the previous day had been taken. Captain Scott, who visited Carnoustie in the course of the day, identified it as that of William Milne. The one who was got on Monday was floating about twelve yards from the beach, two and a half miles West of Carnoustie, and was identified as that of John Hall. It seems that the keeper of the lighthouse saw the boat passing Buddonness. She had put up the sail, and was going at a great rate. A gale of wind accompanied by a heavy shower of rain came on immediately and the keeper then lost sight of the boat. It would appear that the boat had capsized in attempting to round Buddonness Point. This is a 'short cut' which the fishing boats generally take when the water is high . . .

Captain McKinnon picked up on Monday afternoon three oars at the same place as that where the body of the lad Milne was discovered on Tuesday; and Captain Scott identified them as belonging to the boat . . .

Mr Dunbar, Procurator Fiscal, visited Carnoustie, on Tuesday, and made all the investigations possible into the occurrence. The names of the lads and the residences of their mothers (their fathers being all dead) are as follows:–

William Milne, aged fifteen, 138 Hilltown; John Hall, aged fifteen, 9 Annfield Road; William McIntosh, aged thirteen, 11 Annfield Road (body not recovered). On Monday evening when the intelligence became known, the Rev. Mr Piper called on the relatives and acquainted them with the sad circumstances. What object the boys could have had in undertaking their fatal voyage can of course only be guessed at. From their general good conduct, and the fact that as they were almost daily ashore, they had many previous opportunities of escape, it is thought their only intention was to have a sail, and that finding themselves unable to manage the boat, they had attempted to run her ashore, but had found it impossible to do so in consequence of the strong gale and heavy sea.

The storm which had taken the poor souls' boat was not the only storm to rage about the Mars. Was this a tragic accident, was it due to flawed judgement or negligence, or was it a criminal act by the ship's management? The press and the public wanted to have their say. The newspapers had questions to ask and were quickly off the mark:

The narrative on Tuesday of the fatal adventure of the three boys . . . has excited painful interest; and as might be expected, some persons are blaming the officers of the ship for allowing the boys to go ashore without a man in charge of them. It is said that the morning was stormy, that the boat was a small one, and that there should always be one of the officers or crew in every boat that leaves the vessel. We trust that in order to satisfy the public mind there will be no delay in investigating all the circumstances; and we only regret that we have not here, as in England, coroners' inquests, so that such investigations could at once be made public, and that an end might at once be put to exaggerations and misrepresentations which are always current after catastrophes of this kind. It may be well, however, in the meantime to state that although a stiff breeze was blowing from the West on Monday morning, the weather was not at all dangerous for a boat landing from or returning to the Mars; and that the boat in which the five boys were sent ashore as usual for the messages was a strong, safe boat used between the ship and the shore in all kinds of weather. Of course it was never intended for the boys to hoist sail and set out to sea in such a boat; but this the three lads did against the remonstrances of their two companions, who refused to go with them . . .

The suggestion that there should be a man in charge of every boat when it lands naturally presents itself; but an influential member of the Executive Committee to whom we have spoken on the subject says that if the boys were never allowed to go ashore alone it would destroy the moral effect which is gained by trusting to their honour in returning to the ship. Two of the three boys who were drowned were well conducted boys, and had never attempted to run away. The third was also a very active, intelligent boy, and although a little wild had acted as coxswain of one of the boats. All three might have run away any day for the months past, as they were daily going ashore. The Committee have wished to trust the boys in this way as much as they could, and so as to teach them habits of self respect by showing that they were not regarded as wild young vagabonds, who would break away at the first opportunity. If the lads were never allowed to move without a man being along with them, of course they would feel that they were prisoners in charge of a warder's sentinel, or policeman. Moreover, they would get on shore very little compared with that [sic] they now do, as there are often three or four boats away from the ship at a time, and it would be impossible to spare men out of the crew to accompany them without adding considerably to the complement of men on board – which would entail considerable expense. That would, however, be a comparatively unimportant objection if there were not great weight in the contention that it would alter the whole character of the ship if she were to be turned into such a floating prison that the lads could not be trusted ashore except in custody of a man to look after them.

Nothing would be easier for us at this moment than to 'pile up the agony' of lamentation for the loss of these three poor lads, and to denounce the Captain, officers and Committee of the Mars – but let us be just to them, and ask those who may be readiest to condemn them to put themselves in their place. Those who have children of their own must know that it is not always an easy thing to manage half a dozen youngsters without accidents and painful casualties.

How much greater the difficulty of managing between two and three hundred on board a ship, most of whom have been sent there because they were unmanageable on shore? The last man whose position – so full of anxiety and responsibility – is to be envied at any time is that of the Captain of the Mars, and we feel we are only doing what is right in asking that he shall not be condemned unheard.

This seems a balanced view of a highly emotive subject. The loss of boys and men (and women) in factories and at sea, throughout the country, was a daily occurrence. Life, as we have seen (especially among the poor), was cheap. Yet boys in this institution seemed deserving of righteous indignation. It was time for the public to have their say. This letter, from a Dundee solicitor, was written before all the latest news had been published:

March 17th 1871

To the Editor of the Dundee Advertiser

Sir, – A good vessel, a good institution – if well managed – but who in their senses would send five boys in a 'dingy' [sic] with such a wind blowing from the west, when no able-bodied men would go out in search of what is called the 'runaways'? My belief is, they were not runaways but that the boat ran away with them. At all events, no seaman skilled would have sent a dingy out in such a gale with such an infant crew, although it was only to bring back a cargo of red tape letters of little use to anyone. Truly, three little boys were sent through the dead letter office. One has been cast up on the beach, the two

others lie in the deep below the waves. Their names are yet unknown, but they are numbered, and their numbers will never be forgot as long as the Mars lies anchored off Woodhaven.

It is not for me to say a word against the institution. I respect it, but I will not submit to see youths, however bad they may be, sent to their watery graves as these three numbers are gone; and I now put it forcibly if this is the first instance of inhumanity to man on board the Mars? . . .

It is right that the public should know what is done with its children. On behalf of the weeping public, I demand an answer to the following questions:– Why were five such children sent out with the dingy to get letters from the Post Office when no able bodied man would venture out? and who had directed the boys to go on that death errand? . . . If the boys were imprisoned on board the Mars, why were they allowed to go in a boat without an officer in charge? They were sent on board the Mars under a warrant, and without an officer in charge they should not have been allowed to leave the ship, not to speak of the necessity of an able-bodied man going in charge of children sent to sea in a 'dingy'.

The case is one of importance; and when in Edinburgh tomorrow I will take the responsibility of lodging a charge of culpable homicide against some party, leaving the Crown to say who is to blame for the drowning of the three boys.

Need I say more? The above facts speak for themselves. If they are not true let them be contradicted – Your obedient servant.

Arch. Paul

The Captain and the Committee must have been shocked by the tone and intent of this letter. Mr Paul seems justified in his anger at the use of boys to do work in conditions in which *no able bodied man would venture out.* On board the ship, Francis Molison, President of the institution, was holding an inquiry, interviewing some of the boys and Captain Scott to find out what had gone wrong.

It is difficult to think of a sadder sight than the funeral of two of the three boys, William Miln (this is the correct spelling of his name, as it appears this way in his admission page and on the gravestone) and John Hall. (The body of William McIntosh had still not been recovered.)

FUNERAL OF THE TWO MARS BOYS

Friday 17th March

Yesterday at noon the last testimony of respect was paid to the two boys Milne and Hall, who so mournfully perished at the mouth of the Tay on Monday morning . . .

The bodies were placed in cloth-lined coffins, and brought to Dundee by the train arriving at 10 o'clock yesterday. Shortly afterwards they were put into a hearse with plumes, draped in white. Messrs George, James and Thomas Hardy, uncles of the boy

Hall; a brother of the boy Milne; and Mr George Burnett, Mr George Jack, and the Rev. C. A. Piper, accompanied the remains by the 11 o'clock boat from Dundee. On arriving at Newport, the funeral party was met by 104 boys of the Mars, who presented a very striking appearance, being drawn up in two lines, accompanied by the seamen instructors, and under the command of Captain Scott. The boys and instructors uncovered while the hearse was passing, and then formed fours and followed the hearse, preceded by their standard (the Union Jack) half-mast high. After the boys had walked a little over two miles the hearse was stopped about 200 yards from Forgan Churchyard . . .

Two graves were dug on the East side of the churchyard, which is situated in a very sequestered spot, surrounded by some very old yew trees, and in proximity to the ivy-grown ruins of old Forgan Church . . .

The Rev. Mr Thomson offered up a very impressive prayer, feelingly alluding to the melancholy circumstances under which the company were assembled. The Mars boys were formed in two lines behind the chief mourners; and the whole company, who were very much affected, waited till the graves were filled up. The return to the ship was then commenced, the flag being hoisted to the top of the flag pole. The ensign of the Mars was half-mast until the funeral was over, when it was hoisted to the peak.

Mrs Hall came over with the boat, and remained at Newport until the cortege returned.

The gravestone reads:

In memory of William McIntosh, William Miln and John Hall aged respectively 12, 13 and 14 years pupils in the training ship MARS. Who in a fit of waywardness incidental to youth, left Woodhaven pier in an open boat on the stormy morning of March 13th 1871 and were lost on the GAA BANK within one short hour of their sailing.

Their remains were recovered and interred here.

The inscription on the base of the stone reads:

Erected by public subscription collected by John Grant, Woodhaven.

As a last word on this sad event, a poem by Mary Crichton was published at the time, on the finding of the body of John Hall.

'Thou knowst not what a day may bring forth.'
                                        Rom. 1. 37

What means the crowd? Each anxious face
Tells something is ado:
Three boys are drowned, – one body found.
But not the other two.

A stranger quiet to all around,
A lifeless stranger too,
Whose uniform will plainly tell
His friends must have been few.

Behold that calm and pleasant face!
As if in tranquil sleep –
He now lies in Death's cold embrace.
Who perished in the deep.

If there's a mother left behind,
We know that she must feel;
It cannot be an easy task
This message to reveal;–

The boy she brought into the world,
Full fifteen years ago,
Is now to-day a lifeless corpse,
In death's cold arms laid low.

And where is now the immortal soul
While here the body rests?
We cannot tell: let us prepare:
The judge of all knows best.

Mary Crichton, Carnoustie, Dundee

The company of Mars boys, once back on board, may have felt a certain unity after such an emotional experience, which might have been directed against the managers of the ship, or have created a bond between themselves. A month later, one boy showed that bravery was not confined to his masters, the act brought to the attention of the public by a letter from Captain Scott. It seems to have more than a touch of moral justification about it.

To the Editor of the Dundee Advertiser

Sir, The boy Murdoch McLeod fell overboard from the port gangway this morning, when with great presence

57

of mind one of his comrades, Peter McKenna, seized a lifebuoy, leapt overboard, and swam to his assistance. Both boys were picked up none the worst for their ducking. McKenna is about to join the merchant service, and kindly give the occurrence publicity; and I cannot refrain from taking this opportunity of expressing my admiration of the kind and manly hearts of my young charges, as evidenced by constant acts of brotherly love towards each other and daring in their necessarily hazardous training.

I am &c.,

Charles Scott, Captain Superintendent
Mars 19th July 1871

(Considering the height of the Mars from the water, and the strong tide running, this act of Peter McKenna is one of no ordinary gallantry. Peter has long been one of the best lads on board ship – Ed. D.A.)

'The Scum of the Country'

Every year there was a 'visit' to the Mars and a presentation of the accounts for the year. This was a chance for invited guests to congratulate those on board the Mars for the sterling work done during the previous year, and to raise issues relevant to the institution. The meeting in July 1871, in front of a large audience, including all of the Mars boys, was begun with a dry but illuminating speech by the Earl of Dalhousie, who presided:

There were, he found, 217 lads on board the vessel. Of these on admission 20 could read fairly, 22 could read a little, and 175 could not read at all; now 70 could read well, 57 fairly, and 84 a little, while in the column for those who could not read at all there was, he was happy to say, a blank. Then in regard to writing, on admission 184 could not write at all, 23 could write a little, and 10 could write fairly, now 88 could write well, 70 fairly, and 47 a little, and the column for those who could not write at all again appeared to be blank. In Arithmetic, 7 only had a fair knowledge of arithmetic when admitted, 15 a little and 103 were entirely ignorant of figures; now 86 were good at arithmetic, 62 were fair at it, and 43 had a slight knowledge of it; and again he found no column for those who knew nothing. None of the boys had any acquaintance with geography when admitted; now 40 were good at it, 52 had a fair knowledge and 60 had a slight knowledge of it . . .

At the meeting Lord Dalhousie presented Peter McKenna with the medal of the Dundee Humane Society, *they having awarded it to him for having sprung from the deck of the vessel into the water, and thereby saved the life of one of his comrades.*

Next to address the audience, in an outrageously entertaining speech, was the famous Dr Guthrie (of Ragged School fame):

Figure 9 The interior of the tailor's shop on board the Mars in 1907. *(Dundee City Council Central Library)*

Ladies and gentlemen, I have seen no sight more pleasant than that now before me. A set of finer looking, healthier looking lads I have not seen for a long time; and my only regret to-day is this, that I did not bring down in the railway train with me from London a gentleman whom some called the Attorney General and some the Solicitor General, but he was some sort of general or other connected with Australia (Laughter) who chose to make a furious attack upon me when I was very unexpectedly called on to speak in London to a meeting connected with the Colonial Society. On that occasion I recommended the interests of the colonies, because they afforded an admirable outlet to our Ragged School boys – which was greatly cheered at the meeting, and well they might cheer, for our Ragged School boys have proved in Canada and Australia to be the best emigrants these colonies have ever received – when all of a sudden this man leapt upon me like a kangaroo – (Laughter) – and to my astonishment, as well as to the astonishment of the whole meeting, declared that he knew in Australia about ragged school boys, and they were the scum of the country and the worst of the community. Well, whether he was an Attorney-General, or Solicitor-General, or a military general – I don't know there are any naval generals, and what is more, as the honest man said, I don't care. When the late Lord Justice-Clerk Hope was shooting in Ayrshire, he trespassed on the field of an honest farmer who was working among his turnips. Thereupon the farmer ordered him to turn away – he had no right to be there. 'Right to be there?' said he; 'do you know who I am?' 'No,' said the farmer; 'and what's more I don't care.' 'I am the Lord Justice-Clerk.' 'Ye may be onybody's clerk ye like – come oot frae 'mong my neeps.' (Laughter.) Well he may be anybody's general he likes; but as a friend of mine said to me next morning, after he attacked me, he took the wrong dog by the tail. (Laughter.) 'The scum of the country!' I wish I had him here to see these nice fellows before me, looking as well (and I cannot pay them a better compliment) as my own sons . . .

The speech had been quite broadly published and letters were soon flying between newspapers. Dr Guthrie published this in *The Scotsman*:

Dundee, July 31st, 1871

Sir, A friend of mine has sent me a slip from your paper containing a letter from Mr Dutton, Agent-General for the Government of Southern Australia, in which he animadverts on a term that I am made to appear to have applied to Mr Strangeways in a speech I delivered here last Thursday. I hasten to assure Mr Dutton that I have no recollection of applying such an unbecoming term as 'fellow' to that gentleman; that I had no intention of applying such a term to him; and that if I did it, no man could regret it more than I do, but saying this – which is due to myself as well as to one who has the manliness to make no anonymous attack – I seize this opportunity of denouncing anew the rashness and injustice of the Attorney-General of

Australia, or any one else, calling our ragged school children the 'scum of the country', and confounding all such children with some unfortunate, and exceptional, and imperfectly educated specimens that may have been shipped out to Australia. I excused Mr Strangeways on the score of ignorance; but not less did he make an assault on institutions that – to say nothing of the thousands of unhappy children saved from a life of misery, and of the thousands they have sent out into the world to be useful members of society – have done more to repress juvenile crime than all the terrors of lawyers and the law.

I am &c.,

Thomas Guthrie

Before the meeting held on board the Mars, a photograph had been taken of the boys, captain, crew and many important visitors, and as there were no photographs printed in the local papers at the time, they published details of the scene. For possibly the first time, the photograph and the story can be brought together.

PHOTOGRAPH OF THE MARS BOYS

On the morning of the recent public visit to the Mars, the opportunity was taken by Mr Valentine to photograph a numerous group of the boys along with the members of the Committee and the officers of the ship. We have received a copy of a very successful group thus taken. The position selected is immediately before the quarter deck, the boys sitting in the foreground, with the band standing on the left hand –

the Earl of Dalhousie presiding, with Mr Molison, Captain Scott, Messrs Robert Mackenzie, W. W. Renny, R. T. Ferguson, H. Walker, John Shiell, Major Guthrie, on the right hand; Colonel Maitland Dougall, Lieut. Ramsay, Mr Burnett and others on the left. Captain Scott's family are represented on the quarter deck looking over the rail. It is a very striking and pleasing memento of the occasion.

There seems to be confusion of left and right here, with the description of the ship's band standing on the left. As we look at Captain Scott's family, who are pictured standing above, on the quarter deck, we can see two of their boys, C. C. Scott and F. E. Scott, and Captain Scott's wife Agnes, surrounded by her three daughters Caroline, Edith and Lilian. The oldest boy, Augustus, who will return to be Captain, was fourteen and by this time had enrolled in the Navy.

Life on board wasn't all hard work and deck scrubbing. Entertainment was often provided, in the form of lantern shows, concerts and swimming competitions. In this story in the *Dundee Advertiser*, perhaps the boy got the idea from such a swimming match, held the day before, on 21 August 1871:

A BOLD SWIM FROM THE MARS

A very daring escape from the Mars was effected early on Tuesday morning by Murdoch McLeod, the boy whom Peter McKenna recently saved from a watery grave. It appears that McLeod procured a life-buoy, got stealthily into the river, and swam to Newport pier. From this he proceeded to Tayport,

where he was apprehended by Constable Richardson about 2 o'clock the same morning. The constable treated him very kindly, had his clothing dried, and conveyed him to the ship a few hours afterwards. McLeod seemed but little the worse for his long and dangerous swim. He belongs to Woolwich, and was with the ship when she first arrived from England. He states that he was on the watch, and fell overboard. McLeod was one of the boys in the swimming match on the previous evening, but he did not win a medal.

(At this time there was only one Murdoch McLeod on board; might his origins have been recorded mistakenly, or was Murdoch attempting to embellish the truth?)

Escaping from the Mars was not a regular occurrence, although to the young boys it was no doubt a foreign and harsh environment, especially for boys whose backgrounds had had no structure, no discipline, and little or no education. It can't have been easy to make the adjustment from wandering in the streets of Dundee, to life in a full-time educational establishment. Yet the sad reality is that they may have been in a better place than they realised, as life on Scotland's sad streets was not kind.

The Superintendent of the Dundee Police published his report for the year 1871:

The statistics, as a whole, are calculated to deject rather than exhilarate, and there is one piece of information possibly sadder than all the rest. The Superintendent states that 235 applications were made to bury the dead bodies of persons whose relatives could not be found, or were in such destitute circumstances as to be unable to do so. After investigation 18 of the applications were refused, and 217 of the bodies were buried at the expense of the Local Authority. These figures at once present a picture of the life of some of those waifs of society who, wandering far from their homes, are forgotten by their friends, and who, it may be, chiefly by their own misconduct, are in the anguish of despair prompted at last to terminate their existence in places where their individuality had been unknown and unheeded . . .

The number of casual poor who received a night's protection was 297. Thirty-five dogs had been taken to the office, of which 9 had been claimed by their owners and 26 destroyed. Seven boys had been sent by the Magistrates to a reformatory, 14 to industrial schools, and 14 to the Mars Training Ship.

1871

The contract was signed by Charles de Bergue to build the Tay Bridge. His price was £217,099 81s. 6d. On 24 July, W. A. Paterson, a schoolboy, laid the foundation stone at Wormit, Fife.

Figure 10 This picture is reproduced from a photograph taken in 1870, showing the citizens and patrons who were interested in the Mars when she was first brought to Dundee. Among them were Lord Dalhousie, Lord Kinnaird, Sir William Ogilvy Dalgleish, Bart., Admiral Maitland Dougall and many others. *(Fife Council Libraries and Museums)*

4

Law and Disorder

A near riot in the Scouringburn area of Dundee on St Patrick's Day, in 1872, describes the *rowdyism* prevalent in the lawless streets. It would appear that a constable, Peter Forbes, while doing his duty, had apprehended a juvenile up to no good in Lyon's Close and took him in charge. He then attempted to take him to the police office, when he encountered a St Patrick's Day parade, some of whose participants took exception to the policeman's actions.

> *An unusually large number of Irishmen paraded the streets decorated with shamrocks, and in the Scouringburn especially were they in great force. The constables with the boy proceeded down Blackness Road, and by the time they had reached that part of the Scouringburn at the top of Blinshall Street they were surrounded by a crowd numbering several hundreds . . .*

By now, Forbes had been joined by another constable and the confrontation became ugly as blows were struck.

> *Affairs were now beginning to look rather alarming,*

> *as the crowd numbered nearly 2000, and stones, sticks, and mud were being thrown . . .*

The constables did manage to escape, but not before letting go of the young miscreant, with one of the constables nearly having his ear bitten off.

In contrast to these riotous scenes, life on the Mars was beginning to settle into a pattern. It is interesting to look at the admissions to the ship as the number of boys who were on board or had passed through the ship reached 400.

From the beginning of records in October 1869, there had been only four boys admitted from Edinburgh, until a sudden influx, between 20 October 1871 and November 1872, when a further sixty-nine boys were introduced. There were 203 boys from Dundee, eighteen from Fife, ten from Perth, ten from Kirkcaldy, ten from Arbroath, eight from Aberdeen, eight from Ferry Port on Craig, six from Cupar, five from Montrose, four from St Andrews, three from Stirling, two from Brechin, one from Banff, one from Galashiels, one from Linlithgow, one from Newport and two from London. (The remaining boys had no home address or District Court designation noted on their admission page.)

Out of the records available, where religious persuasion is given, of those 300 boys, 240 were Protestant and sixty were Roman Catholic. These figures were to change dramatically in the years to come.

The Edinburgh Committee for the Mars was very active. A meeting was held at the Royal Hotel on 22 February 1872, the proceedings having been opened with prayer by the Rev. Mr Cullen, Admiral Sir W. Hope Johnstone presiding:

The Chairman reminded the meeting that a few years ago an attempt was made to procure a training ship for the Firth of Forth. Considerable promises of support were got, but after looking at the expense that would be incurred, it was found that sufficient funds were not likely to be forthcoming, and with some hesitation the project was dropped, at all events for the time. When, however, the Dundee people obtained the Mars, they very generously said that, provided some support was raised in Edinburgh for that ship, they would receive a number of boys from this quarter. A deputation from the managers of the Mars was now present to explain the success which had attended their undertaking.

Mr Harris said the directors of the Mars had behaved in a most generous manner. Instead of stipulating that any fixed sum should be raised by Edinburgh friends, they had offered to take any number of boys that were found suitable, leaving the raising of funds an open question. Annual subscriptions to the amount of £100 had been promised, but he hoped that next year that would be doubled, seeing that 56 boys had already been sent from Edinburgh to the training ship.

The *Lightning*, and later the *Francis Molison*, were the Mars tenders, masted sailing ships which were used to train boys in seamanship, and in the summer they sailed around Britain. The *Lightning* in 1873 was lying off Granton near Edinburgh, where the boys performed for an audience of visitors and spectators.

The Mars band played a selection of music for their entertainment. After refreshments had been taken by the visitors, a meeting was held between decks. Among those present were – Dr Alexander Wood, president of the Association for Improving the Condition of the Poor; Governor Smith of the Calton Prison; Mr David Harris, Hon. Secretary of the Edinburgh Industrial Brigade; Colonel Robeson, United States Consul; Councillors Donald and Mitchell and Councillor A. Clark of Leith; Mr Thomas Knox, ex-Master of the Merchant Company; Mr John Greig, Hon. Secretary in Edinburgh of the Mars Training Ship Institution; Mr Renny (of the Dundee Committee); Captain Crichton, R.N., Edinburgh; Dr Moir, Rev. Dr Gordon of St Mary's, Grosvenor Square, London; Mr Robert Campbell, and a number of ladies.

At the meeting Mr Smith, Governor of Calton Prison, said:

He had no doubt the experiment which had been made in establishing the Mars Training Ship was one in the right direction, and one which could not fail of success. He had great faith in getting hold of these boys at an early period of their life to save them from crime. Since he first considered this subject, he had been struck with the fact that in 1847, when the Original Ragged School was established, there had been committed in Edinburgh 560 lads between 14 and 16 years of age, whilst last year the number had been only 80. This he regarded as a most instructive fact as to the effect of such institutions. The convictions during the same period had been reduced from 5? per cent, to under 1 per cent. (Cheers.) . . .

Captain Scott, in returning thanks, said all he wanted was that they would send him the boys. These 'waifs and strays' made splendid sailors. He gave an account of what took place on the night of the terrible thunderstorm, on 22nd July, when he went to sea with the boys. On that occasion they had not shown the slightest fear, though the storm was such as to strike terror into the most courageous heart, but had discharged their duty in a manner that would have done credit to any body of men. (Cheers.)

The bond between Edinburgh and the Mars Institution was to be sorely tested over the next few years, as serious allegations were made concerning the admission of boys to the ship and their treatment on board. The argument seems to have been between ex-Baillie Lewis from Edinburgh, who had received certain information against the ship, and Mr Thomas Knox (a great advocate of the ship) and the Mars Committee. (Ex-Baillie Lewis and Mr Knox were both members of the Edinburgh Parochial Board.)

On 11 April Mr Knox wrote to *The Scotsman*:

Sir, – In the recent unpleasant controversy I have endeavoured to think much of the Mars and little of self. The conduct of the public men is always impartially judged and appraised in the long run. Surprises and misrepresentations may prevail for a brief period, but not always. The true only appears truer by trial and inquiry, but the false even falser.

And what is true regarding individuals is equally so with institutions. Accordingly, the Mars, in spite of the recent avalanche of defamatory epithets, will more conspicuously than ever stand forth to public view as one of the noblest institutions for the rescue of unhappy boys from the ways of crime and vice that this or any country owns by sea or land . . .

It is a work which cannot fail to command the interest and excite sympathy of all who love to serve God in the way of saving those who are ready to perish. Such facts, such bright and hopeful results, are a silver lining in the dark cloud of city juvenile depravity. Such moral, social, and industrial facts are indeed a finger-post on the wayside of society, telling our municipal authorities and our imperial governments the road to follow clear of the expense and disgrace of poorhouses, prisons, penitentiaries, and hulks.

I am, &c.,

Thomas Knox

The accusation that had been levelled at the Mars Committee by ex-Baillie Lewis, was that irregular procedure had been used in the admission of the boy John (or James) Walker, and that *boys had been tied to the guns, and lashed and scourged.* If this was true, it was indeed a serious matter. It would appear that the information had been taken from certain Mars boys and given in evidence to Mr Lewis. The language between the parties at times became quite vitriolic, including accusations of *kidnapping of boys off the streets of Edinburgh.*

A letter appeared in *The Scotsman* on 25 April 1874, signed W. W., and as it obviously came from the Mars 'camp', it may have been written by W. W. Renny, Vice-President of the Mars Institution. The tone of the letter is difficult to fathom at first reading, until you read it as a method of poking fun at the 'outrageous' allegations brought by ex-Baillie Lewis.

> *Sir – I have been much gratified of late by observing the deep interest shown by the City Parochial Board for the poor children who have in vast numbers been kidnapped by Justices of the Peace, often with the consent of their parents, and illegally imprisoned in certified Industrial Schools, under the special direction of her Majesty's Home Secretary, who employ inspectors to visit the schools, and report yearly whether everything therein is conducted according to law. But it appears that all the officials, Secretary of State, magistrates, and inspectors, have for a long time been giving their sanction to most illegal proceedings, by irregularly committing poor friendless children to certified Industrial Schools, and detaining them therein against their wish and the wishes of their bereaved parents . . .*
>
> *I am &c.,*
>
> *W. W.*

A letter with so much humour seems to indicate a certain amount of confidence that the allegations are totally groundless, though this was to prove slightly premature, as the government inspectors now made a move to stop any more irregularities. Their letter was read out at a meeting of the Edinburgh Parochial Board, where at least some of them were proud of their involvement in this case, though others were not so sure:

> *Home Secretary*
>
> *Sir, – With reference to the memorial from the Edinburgh City Parish Parochial Board, dated 27th April, on the subject of irregular procedure in the case of James Walker, committed to the 'Mars' training ship, I am instructed by Mr Secretary Cross to state for the information of the Board that measures have been taken to prevent the recurrence of the irregularities complained of, and that the committals under the Industrial Schools Act will not take place in future except after public investigation in open court.*
>
> *Henry Selwin Ibbetson.*

Ex-Baillie Lewis was quick to seize upon this partial success, saying that

> *the letter had shown the wisdom of the action taken up by the Board, as not only had there been a saving to the Board of the money involved in this particular case, but, as previously indicated, that case might have presented a precedent that might have involved an expenditure of several hundred pounds per annum . . .*
>
> *Another Mr Lewis – Mr James Lewis – did not wish to reopen this matter now, but he would say that this letter had not saved them one penny. They were in the same position as before, still charged with claim for the boy Walker.*

It would appear that the high profile now attached to this case was beginning to have an effect on other members of the Board. Ex-Baillie Lewis seems to have become slightly isolated in his constant attacks on the Mars management.

Mr Miller thought it was a pity that any discussion should have been raised on this subject after this satisfactory letter from the Home Office. (Hear, hear.) It had been assumed by some that he and some of the Board who had taken action in this matter were opposed to the system of training ships. This was not the case; on the contrary, he had been in favour of them very strongly. (Hear, hear.) They had objected merely to the irregular manner in which the law had been dispensed – (Hear, hear.) – and he hoped, now that the law had been satisfactorily vindicated by Government, a very large number of boys would be sent to the ship in accordance with the law. (Hear, hear.)

The Mars Committee may have felt that it was now time to attempt to limit the damage done to the ship's reputation by this scandal, and so a detailed letter was sent to ex-Baillie Lewis in August 1874 from the Mars's secretary George Jack. In it he tries to explain the procedure, and record of punishment, on board the ship:

As regards punishment for grave offences, boys are punished in a similar manner to that common in every public school. The 'taws', such as is common in all schools, is almost always used. At times they have been punished with a birch rod, being a more lenient mode of punishment than the taws for smaller boys, and all punishments are carried out very formally in presence of the officers of the ship. During the year 1873, out of 305 boys, 6 boys were punished with from 7 to 18 stripes. The two boys who got 18 stripes were punished for a serious offence, and one of these, since he has joined the Royal Navy, has sent a warmly expressed letter of thanks to Captain Scott for his good treatment and kindness. Since October 1873 to this time, there has only been one punishment of six stripes. There is a regular register of punishments on board the Mars, which has been certified as approved by the Rev. Sydney Turner, Inspector of Industrial Schools, and Mr Rogers, his assistant.

Of the boys discharged from the Institution 166 have joined the Royal Navy or merchant service, and 57 have gone to occupations on shore. The latter, in most instances, were influenced by depraved relatives to go to shore occupations, that they might get the proceeds of the boys' labours: but it has been ascertained that two thirds of them at least afterwards went to sea. It must also be remembered that a considerable number of the boys admitted into the Institution are found unfit for seafaring life from weak constitutions.

The Executive Committee would ask you to visit the Institution. Come any day without any previous announcement, live a week on board, and then report your impressions of the work that is being done.

I am Sir your obedient servant,
                                    G. Jack, Secretary to the Institution

Ex-Baillie Lewis replied from Roselea Villa, Grange, Edinburgh, on 21 August 1874. In a slightly more conciliatory manner than previously, he says:

I have in the first place to correct a misapprehension which appears to exist in your minds, viz.:– that I am opposed to the Mars Training Ship as an industrial institution. I am not surprised that you should entertain such an idea, in view of the unworthy and persistent attempts which have been made in certain quarters to convey such an impression to the public mind. I have hitherto refrained from correcting these misrepresentations; feeling satisfied that my antecedents and public life, extending over a period of more than twenty years, rendered such a refutation unnecessary on my part . . .

Once again, he outlines his argument relating to the *illegal* method of admission of boys from Edinburgh:

I confess that when I reflect that while the said J.P. [Mr Knox] was dispensing his sentences and warrants of committal in private there was no public prosecutor, police constable, nor clerk of court present, and that no record of the form of the procedure was kept for the satisfaction of the parents or the public; and further, when I reflect that all this was being done in secret, without the knowledge of the citizens or the press, I feel that it would have been treason to the interests of the community and to the rising youth of the city had I remained silent in these circumstances.

A reply, in the form of a newspaper article, shows a hardening attitude towards the ex-Baillie, while accepting that there were failings on the Mars; it also mentions another argument which may have been behind the whole affair:

Ex-Baillie Lewis, in his plausible reply to Mr Jack, makes it apparent that his object is rather to strike at Mr Knox – with whom since the Edinburgh Water Contest he has been at war – than at the Mars as an Institution. There is no doubt that in point of form Mr Knox was technically wrong in signing warrants for the commitment of a certain number of boys to the Mars on one side of the street in Edinburgh rather than the other – in his own premises rather than the Court . . .

It is doubtful whether all this noise about the Manner in which these warrants were signed would have been made but for the opportunity it gave the ex-Baillie of annoying one of the most philanthropic men in Edinburgh, with whom he has had a local feud . . . Now Captain Scott does not profess to maintain discipline of the ship without occasionally inflicting punishment. So far, however, from it being the fact that the boys are cruelly treated, it is a very remarkable feature in the government of the ship that discipline is admirably maintained with so small an amount of punishment. On this subject we have more reliable authority than Mr Lewis, who owns that he brought his grave charge merely 'on the statements of boys who have waited on him'.

It would seem that nothing would end this row; no amount of attack and defence seemed to resolve the problem. A visit to the ship on 31 August 1874, not by the ex-Baillie, but by the Lords of the Admiralty, was to prove crucial to the outcome:

After they had visited H.M.S. Unicorn, *Camperdown Works and Baxter's Works the Mars boys formed in two lines on the deck in their white shirts, blue bonnets and trousers they were ready to be inspected by Mr Ward Hunt, Admiral Tarleton and Captain Seymour, and after a series of drills with the band at their head playing a grand march they marched in fours around the deck. Their Lordships inspected the school, the ship's sanitary conditions, and on returning to the upper deck the attention of the visitors was attracted to a very fine globe, recently presented to the ship by an anonymous donor. The method of teaching the boys steering by the points of the compass with a model ship moving on a pivot was also witnessed. A visit to the library completed the inspection of the ship. The party then proceeded to the cabin, where luncheon was provided.*

In absence of Mr Molison of Errol Park, the President of the Institution, Mr W. W. Renny, the Vice-President, took the chair – Captain Scott, of the Mars, acting as croupier. There were also present the Right Hon. G. Ward Hunt, Admiral Tarleton, Captain Seymour, R.N., Captain Brome, R.N., Captain W. H. Maitland-Dougall of Scotscraig; Captain Traill, of the Local Marine Board; Mr Yeaman, M.P. for Dundee; Provost Cox; Mr George Burnett; Mr Robert Mackenzie; Mr John Leng, and the Rev. C. A. Piper. After the health of Her Majesty had been drunk with all her honour,

The CHAIRMAN said it gave the Committee much pleasure to receive the Lords of the Admiralty on board the Mars, and especially to know that they had been so much satisfied with what they had witnessed that day. The Committee did not shrink from every part of the ship, its management and discipline being examined by those who were so well qualified to judge of the manner in which everything was conducted and the results attained on board . . .

Mr Ward Hunt, in reply, said that during their visits to the various rivers and seaports they inspected a number of Training Ships, and he was gratified in being able to state that they found none in a more satisfactory condition than the Mars. The general appearance of the ship and the boys was all that could be desired. The writing and the reading of the boys were remarkably good. He especially commended the gun drill, as showing that such ships might be made useful training schools for the navy and valuable auxiliaries to the mercantile marine. The large bath in the fore part of the ship was a

Figure 11 The boys at Woodhaven with the ship's tender, *Francis Molison*, going through their various drills, including bridge-building between the two piers. *(Dundee Art Galleries and Museums)*

peculiarity of the Mars well worth copying on board similar ships . . .

What he had seen reflected great credit on Capt. Scott and on the Committee, whom he thanked for their attention that day.

. . . This brought the proceedings to an end, and the company having embarked on board the Excelsior, an Admiral's salute of nineteen guns was fired by the juvenile gunners on board the Mars in excellent style.

This would seem to be a clean bill of health as far as the Mars and the Admiralty were concerned, and may have put an end to the acrimonious dispute, a fact that *The Scotsman* pointed out on 2 September:

The high praise which the Lords of the Admiralty bestowed upon the Mars Training Ship, when they visited it on Monday, may lead some people to wonder what all the bother about the ship which there has been in Edinburgh has meant. Briefly put, the answer to any question of that kind must be, that all the noise has been the production of one person, who has no hesitation about means so long as he keeps himself posturing as a patriot before the community.

There was no excuse for the use of such terms as 'kidnapping'; and there was equally no justification for language which, whether it was intended or not, appeared to reflect on the management of the Mars, and was calculated to injure discipline on board the ship.

The article continues as a personal attack on ex-Baillie Lewis, without mentioning him by name:

It may be safely inferred that if the stories thus told to him were true or would bear examination, they would be told to those who had the power to remedy them. Is the room which he occupies as a public servant constituted his Cave, where what appears to be a willing ear is lent to stories to the disparagement of other people? . . .

The Mars authorities, however, have no reason to trouble themselves with accusations coming from such a source. Everybody who has seen the ship and the discipline aboard of it speak of them in the highest terms. Mr Ward Hunt did not stint in his commendation. Under these circumstances, the attacks of our resuscitated self-constituted censor, based on back stairs stories told by persons of more than doubtful character, may be safely disregarded.

One last (undated) article from the cuttings book at the Blyth Hall in Newport is undoubtedly on the same subject, and a lid is finally put on this particular can of worms:

Edinburgh people should surely be ashamed to see a well-paid Treasurer of one of their endowed schools setting himself to inflame the minds of the parents and friends of the boys on board the Mars Training Ship against Captain Scott and the Committee. If Baillie Lewis had to manage three hundred boys of the class of the Mars boys we very much doubt whether, at the end of several years of his superintendence, he would be held in the same esteem as Captain Scott is by all who are in the habit of visiting the Mars, or whether the great majority of the boys on board would have occasion to entertain towards him the same grateful feelings.

Ex-Baillie Lewis must have felt a lonely voice against what appeared to be a well-respected institution. All his accusations seem to have been dealt with, or found to be groundless. It may be cold comfort to supply a little new information. An interview with an ex-Mars boy, Murdoch McLeod, who would have been aboard ship around the time of the furore, reports:

Iron discipline was maintained on the Mars in those years, and many a time he was slung across the cannon which had roared in battle before the Mars was removed from the list of men-o'-war, and lashed with a rope's end.

Perhaps ex-Baillie Lewis wasn't as far off the mark as he seemed.

Despite the public brouhaha, admissions to the ship continued to come from all over Scotland. The following are just a few of them.

Aberdeen Journal, *1872*

Yesterday, two boys, named respectively James Fairweather and James Ross were brought before D. R. L. Grant, Esq., and James Chivas Esq., Justices of the Peace, at the instigation of the Chief Constable of the County, being wanderers without any feasible means of subsistence, and ordered to be sent to the Mars.

Glasgow Herald, *1884*

Portobello –

At the Portobello Police Court yesterday a boy named Edward Crossley, 12 years of age, was sent to the Mars Training Ship for 4 years for having begged on Brighton Crescent. It was mentioned that the lad's mother was separate from her husband, and had a family of five hanging on her hands. Another boy named Peter Cochrane, was sent to the Mars Training Ship for 3 years, it being proved to the satisfaction of the Magistrate (Baillie Thomson) that he was uncontrollable, and would not go to school.

Aberdeen Weekly Journal, *1893*

A CURIOUS DEATH-BED REQUEST

In the Leith Police Court on Saturday morning a Newhaven boy named Bachelor was brought before the Magistrate as having been found wandering without proper guardianship. A witness, an old woman, stated that the boy's father on his death-bed requested that the lad should be sent to the Mars Training Ship. An officer of the Society for Prevention of Cruelty to Children, which had instituted proceedings, having explained that the Mars authorities had expressed willingness to receive the boy, the Magistrate ordered him to be kept on that vessel till he was 16 years of age.

Another boy, James Robertson, from Newport, on 12 May 1883 simply turned up at the Mars's 'doorstep' at Woodhaven, and asked *to be taken, as he had no home.*

Getting on the Mars was not difficult, but getting off the ship was a different matter altogether. Escaping was one way. Applying to the Captain, through the appropriate channels, was another possibility. More often than not, applications were turned down flat, but from the minute books, here are two with positive conclusions:

1888

An application from the mother of boy Croll was read to have him discharged on licence and placed in another school.

This application was very fully and carefully considered. The Committee had never exercised their powers in this respect and did not wish to encourage applications of this nature, but taking into consideration the circumstances of this case they resolved to grant the application of Mrs Croll subject in all respects to the conditions specified in the Industrial Schools Act as to licensing boys, and also provided that Mr Moncur and Captain Crowdace, after personal enquiry, shall report favourably to the Secretary.

The boy was released on licence and attended Balfour Street School.

1889

There was read a letter from Captain Scott representing that boys Donald McPhail and A. L. Maurice had friends in Canada and [sic] were

desirous to have the boys there, and that the boys were anxious to go, and asking whether the boys might be allowed to go. – No outfit would be required, and the passage would be about 6 guineas each, the Committee considered the matter and thought it well to send the boys as requested.

Captain Scott's 'craves'

Captain Scott's thoughtful side comes over in the words of the Mars minute books, where he 'craves' additional supplies for his boys, including:

. . . extra woollen comforters and a crave from Captain Scott was read, asking the Committee to authorize the purchase of 60 pairs of slippers from Old Mill Reformatory, at Aberdeen at 2/- per pair, for the use of boys with tender feet.

Captain Scott represented that he had found that the serge trousers supplied to the boys while very good for the greater part of the year had not sufficient warmth for the winter season, and recommended that a supply of trousers of a heavier make should be allowed against next winter.

. . . Captain Scott represented the necessity of increasing the supply of books on board the Mars. Suitable books of this kind were indispensable both for amusing the boys and giving them a taste for reading.

Captain Scott's duties were complex and numerous. Not only was he concerned with the discipline of the boys and men, but he was in overall charge of every detail, from dealing with the silting up of the moorings, to the purchasing of supplies, the heating and maintenance of the ship, and the health and safety of everyone on board. Even while he was away from the ship, often when on holiday, he would use the time to attempt to find berths for his boys. On a visit to Portsmouth in 1878, while on duty on the *Lightning*, he successfully placed four Mars boys on HMS *Vincent*, for which the ship received £100 capitation grant from the Admiralty. He would often attend meetings and conferences, dealing with the ever-changing rule amendments which regularly affected the Mars.

He seems genuinely committed to getting the best for the ship, though in one instance he also seemed to profit. In 1873 the minute book notes:

Captain Scott reported that the tenant of the public house at Woodhaven having received notice to quit, and it being rumoured that the place was to be let as a coffee house which would prove an even greater nuisance to this Institution than it had previously been, he at once in his own responsibility made an offer for the premises as an occasional residence for his family who were suffering from so much confinement on board, and for other purposes connected with the Institution. The rent was £40 per annum but by careful management the large garden attached to the house might be made to return the money in supplying vegetables to the ship, and submitted that the Committee might approve of what he had done.

When the ship was visited by eighty Reformatory Officials who were attending a conference in Edinburgh, the seeming informality shows a confidence in the boys under Captain Scott's stewardship.

Undoubtedly Mr Thomas Knox had been the instigator of this visit, and his health was drunk at the luncheon on board *in consideration of his disinterested efforts in connection with the ship.*

After luncheon, the visitors dispersed themselves over the ship, examined her fittings, chatted with the boys, and made themselves acquainted with their every day life – the band, meanwhile, which was stationed on the poop, discoursing pleasant music. After a time, the boys, clean, trig [sic], and smiling, were mustered on the main deck, where they were put through the carbine and other drill by one of the officers. Then came a boat race, in which two of the ship's pinnaces were engaged, and in which much muscle and skill were displayed; then more drill, and at length 'skylarking', which meant several hundred boys scouring the deck in all directions, mounting the shrouds, playing hide-and-seek, or doing anything their fancy suggested. During this relaxation of discipline, a most enjoyable concert was got up, Mr Knox leading off with 'Harry Bluff' and 'Tom Bowling', in the choruses of which the boys joined lustily. Next came a nautical song with a whistling chorus, given by the boys in concert; which, again, was followed by a harmonium solo with a whistling accompaniment, amusingly rendered by one of the visitors . . .

Special visitors

As mentioned above, the building of the ill-fated railway bridge over the Tay had a big effect, both directly and indirectly, on day-to-day life on board. The busy river traffic and both banks milling with construction workers were a constant source of diversion to the boys. Not only would the bridge bring prosperity to Dundee and the North, but the physical presence of the structure would break up the ice floes that so often threatened the Mars in winter. The bridge attracted visitors from all over the world, including Pedro II, Emperor of Brazil. The Emperor was passionately interested in the education of the young and is recorded as having said that, if he had not been Emperor of Brazil, he would like to have been a schoolteacher. Although he must have seen the ship on his visit to the bridge, unfortunately he did not stop for a visit.

However on Saturday, 1 September 1877, a train from Edinburgh stopped at Tayport at 11.33. Had it been raining, the occupants would have gone directly to the bridge, but as the sun was shining brightly, it was decided that, after a considerable railway journey, all concerned would prefer a sail to the bridge. The party, now on board the *Excelsior*, had simply intended to visit the railway bridge, but our old friend Mr Knox (Secretary of the Edinburgh branch of the Mars Institution) suggested to Lord Provost Falshaw of Edinburgh that their guests might wish to visit the Mars. At his instigation and to the complete surprise of the Captain, crew and boys of the Mars, the *Excelsior*, instead of returning the salute of the boys as they sailed past, pulled up alongside the ship, the band struck up 'Yankee Doodle Dandy', and the bearded, blue-coated, General Ulysses S. Grant, ex-President of the United States of America, his wife and son, stepped aboard the Mars Training Ship.

The visit to the bridge had been much publicised, and the Mars was appropriately bedecked and decorated with flags from stem to stern, the yards being manned, and the rail netting lined by the young sailors:

When the ex-President stepped on board, the band, led by Mr Tero, struck up the 'German War Song', and during the hour over which the visit extended a varied selection of music was performed. Shortly after all the visitors had reached the Mars, at a given signal the boys left their places on the rail and yards and mustered in divisions on the upper deck. General and Mrs Grant conversed briefly with several of the lads and subsequently went round most of the ship exploring 'tween decks, Captain Scott explaining the nature of the work performed by the boys and the general details of the training. The veteran soldier expressed his satisfaction with the sailor-like bearing of the boys, and seemed particularly pleased with the activity and tidy appearance presented by the cook's assistant. A very minute inspection of the vessel having been made, the party returned to the upper deck. There all hands were assembled, and, led by Mr Nichols, the 'Canadian Boat Song' was capitally given. Mrs Grant appeared delighted with the fresh, sweet voices of the boys and joined with them in the song. Before it was finished the fire bell was rung, and the youngsters instantly scampered off to their respective posts, manned the fire-engines, and had the hose in readiness in a couple of minutes. The alacrity displayed by the boys, the cool and collected manner in which every one went about their duty, the absence of all confusion, and the perfect quietness were admired and commented upon. The hose and other apparatus having been replaced at the word of command, the boys were drawn up on both sides of the deck.

Lord Provost Falshaw then said – I have to thank Captain Scott for his kindness to-day in showing us over the Mars, and I hope he and his good lady will accompany us to the Tay Bridge. (Cheers.)

Captain Scott replied – I esteem it a great honour to have been visited by General Grant and the Lord Provost of Edinburgh, and I am certain that the visit will be remembered with pleasure by every one on board. (Cheers.)

Lord Provost Falshaw, addressing the boys, then said – Here is a great General – General Grant, from America – come to see you, and I am sure what he would say to you would be – obedience; pay attention to those who are above you, and fulfil all the duties incumbent on you; and mind, since you have great privileges, you have also great responsibilities. (Cheers.) You must all strive to rise to be good men and useful members of society. (Cheers.)

Ex-Provost Cox – There may be Generals amongst them. (Renewed cheers.)

Lord Provost Falshaw – If there are not Generals amongst you, boys, there will be many corporals amongst you at least. (Cheers.) You will all get on by good conduct, and steady, patient perseverance. (Cheers.)

An unbelievable and unforgettable experience, for both boys and men on board, and a piece of great opportunism by Mr Thomas

Knox. Sadly, Mr Knox was to die on 4 December 1879. His funeral took place in Edinburgh on the 9th:

> *The remains were followed to their last resting place in the Grange Cemetery by several hundreds of leading citizens and representatives of public and other bodies with which the deceased gentleman was connected. Admiral Maitland Dougall of Scotscraig, Captain Scott, Admiralty Instructor Betsworth, Instructor Stovin and forty boys from the Mars Training Ship were present by special invitation and headed the funeral cortege from the residence of the gentleman to the place of interment.*

The Mars minute book for December 1879 mentions the sad death of Thomas Knox, though there is no mention of an even greater catastrophe.

The Tay Bridge disaster

This dreadful event was probably as poignant for the small boys on the Mars as it was for many throughout the nation. The boys would have daily looked upon its progress, and have been caught up in the excitement of its imminent official opening. They would have watched the thin pillars grow out of the stormy waters, and marvelled at the raising of the high girders. The boys were even the happy recipients of the goodwill of a gentleman's club, founded, ostensibly, to cater for the bridge managers working on the new bridge, including the Superintendent Engineer, A. Grothe. The club in Newport-on-Tay was situated at the junction of West Road and Cuthbert's Brae and was also known as 'The Private Club', or even, uncharitably, 'The Den of Vice'. It regularly donated old newspapers and periodicals for the men and boys on board. Apart from the daily newspapers, *The Graphic, The Strand*, the *Illustrated London News, Black and White* and *Punch* were all passed on. These gentlemen, and the rest of the inhabitants of Dundee, had watched Christmas come and go, with all the usual amusements available at the time. They had a choice of the *magnificent pantomime, 'Little Bo-Peep', at the Theatre, an attractive company at the Music Hall, and the Waxwork in Lindsay Street Hall; plus Tannakar's Japanese Troupe and Hamilton's Panorama . . .*

The story of the fateful night is retold by the Mars's carpenter, Alexander McDougall:

Probably the most memorable day of all my fifty years on the Mars was that on which the bridge fell and the Edinburgh train was dashed to its doom in the river. It was the night of the 28th of December 1879, and blowing a hurricane. Half of the Mars' officers were on shore as usual, Captain Scott and I went forward on the upper deck and I went forward to look at the moorings. While we were forward there I well remember that we made the remark to one another that we should not like to cross the bridge in the train that night.

Shortly after that I was looking over the starboard side, and I thought I saw a vacant space in the bridge. I went to get the Captain's binoculars, and through them, sure enough I could see the 14 stumps of the wrecked pillars, but no trace of bridge or girders . . . We learned, however, that the Edinburgh train had gone.

Then Captain Scott said to me, 'Do you think you can go round the bridge?' I said we could, and with four men and two boys we set out, taking lifebuoys and spirits with us in case of rescue work. We rowed up and passed the bridge. In the moonlight we could see the tops of the girders and the hanging ruins at the south side of the gap. We crossed to Craig Pier, and reported to the men gathered there what we had seen. Then we set out for the Mars again, arriving there at two in the morning, five hours after we had set out. We had been given up for lost.

Captain Scott testified to the Board of Trade Inquiry, set up to look at the causes of the disaster:

The railway officials are blamed for permitting the train to go up on the bridge during such a hurricane as prevailed on Sunday evening. Captain Scott, of the Training Ship Mars, which is stationed a few hundred yards below the bridge, near the Fife shore, was observing the structure during the evening while the gale was rising. If the storm increased in violence he expected every moment, he states, to see the bridge give way, and he never imagined for a moment that any attempt would be made to take the train across. About seven o'clock he was watching a train with his night glass, but from the position of his vessel he failed to see the light of the train when it entered the bridge . . .

Figure 12 The 400 Mars boys in 1908. The group is arranged on the after part of the quarterdeck and on the poop. *(Dundee City Council Central Library)*

The day after the disaster the Mars was visited by investigators, seeking their accounts of the previous night's storm and aftermath. On that solemn day, from first light there were over a hundred ships on the Tay, looking for any signs of life, then as time wore on, only for bodies:

While the operations were in progress a number of boats came out on the river. The Mars boys launched one of their cutters, and followed Captain Scott and his son to the Fairweather. *Captain Scott suggested to Captain Robertson that he might go across the fallen girders with his cutter and take soundings with the lead and sounding poles, and see whether he could not in this way learn where the train lay. His juvenile crew bravely rowed him about, and showed great eagerness to assist those engaged in the search as far as they possibly could. Captain Scott ran between each of the fallen piers, and stated that he met with something about six feet under water between the third and fourth piers, which he believed to be the unfortunate train.*

The sound and fury which followed the fall of the bridge took many forms, and some strange theories attended, one of which was the possible murder, on the Newport shore, of Annie Cruickshanks, the first body from the train wreck to be found. Another, which would rage on for some time, was that the fall of the bridge was an Act of God, for breaking the Sabbath. Yet the most heart-rending letters were from the families of the victims, who were becoming increasingly concerned over the lack of bodies being recovered. This letter explains the deep frustration and passion felt at the time.

The recovery of bodies

To the editor of the Dundee Advertiser

Sir – Eight days have now elapsed, and only four bodies have been got by man's exertions. Truly the long suffering patience of the public, especially of the bereaved, is being sorely tried. Evidently the Directorate of the North British Company is so engrossed with defending their money interests and planning the rebuilding of their fallen structure that they cannot give time, thought, or attention to the question how best may the dead be restored to their sorrowing friends. In the name of outraged feeling I thus publicly call upon the Directors (1) to appoint a thoroughly competent and well-skilled engineer to take full charge of the operations now being carried on at the bridge; and (2) to secure at once the services of a goodly number of steam trawlers, and a fair and honest chance given us of burying our dead. The North British Railway Company is sometimes spoken of as a headless concern. Let not its management conjoin therewith a heartlessness the most brutal – I am &c.,

One of the Mourners
Dundee, 6th January 1880

The Mars remained, geographically at least, at the centre of all the bizarre attempts to find bodies. For example, they had the idea to fire cannon from either side of the river so that the concussion would assist bodies to float to the surface. Dynamite was also suggested by Mr James Turner, *for Nobel's Explosives Co., 62 Commercial Street, Dundee.* On one occasion an explosion did blow a large Newfoundland dog out of the water and high into the air, *but it was not believed to have been in the train at the time of the disaster.* For ships engaged in the search, a bounty per body found was announced, but the method they eventually used might have left a few on board the Mars, who must have watched it in action, a little unsettled.

14 January 1880

THE TRAWLING OPERATIONS

The small amount of success which had attended the efforts of the whaling and volunteer boat crews in their search of the river for bodies during the last few days have caused some uneasiness in the public mind, and various schemes have been suggested for a systematic search being prosecuted. The North British Railway Company, wishing to do all they can for the recovery of the bodies of the unfortunate victims, have carefully considered the suggestions offered, and they have now practically placed the work of the recovery of the bodies in the hands of Mr Waddell, who has already contracted to raise the fallen girders. [A trawl was therefore commissioned.]

This trawl, which was made at the Dundee Harbour Works, is of novel construction. A thick beam forty feet in length has been procured, and at distances of about three feet apart fifteen pieces of rope, each thirty feet long, are tied, large grapnels being fastened to the ends of the ropes. The grapnels are formidable looking instruments, have been specially made for the work, and are so sharp in the prongs that they will sink six or eight inches into the sand while being dragged along the bed of the river. Every grapnel has four prongs, is between two and three feet long, and two feet broad over the prongs. This trawl was placed on one of the Dundee Harbour Trustees' crane barges yesterday morning, and about eight o'clock the barge, on which was Captain Robertson, the Harbourmaster, Mr Waddell, jun., the Harbour Trustee's diving squad, four dockgatemen, and the crews of two whale boats, left the Tidal Basin in tow of the steamer Unity for the Bridge . . . [After several attempts had been made] *nothing had been hooked, except for an old boot and an unfortunate flounder . . . A third trawl was made between the Mars and the Newport shore to no avail . . . When the barge was turned about three hundred yards east of the third pier and the trawl was hoisted it was observed that one body had been hooked by one of the grapnels. The crews of several boats that were lying alongside at once lent a hand, and the body – that of a young man – was got on board a whale boat . . .*

One body was found for which they would get no bounty – the body of a Mars boy. On the afternoon of Tuesday, 13 January 1880:

The body of a Mars boy who was drowned while stepping off a boat at the ship on a stormy night some weeks ago was found in the Tay. While the ferry steamer was about half way across on its way to Dundee between four and five o'clock Stewart Carrie who was at the wheel, observed the body. The vessel was at once stopped and a boat manned by two of the crew and three passengers put off and recovered the remains of the poor lad, which were taken to the deadhouse at Dundee. Deceased's name was William Young. He was 15 years of age.

This perfectly illustrates the difficulties facing those involved in raising the bodies from the treacherous river currents, as poor William Young had fallen from a boat by the ship on 28 November. It appeared, from the minute books, that he had fallen into the water and immediately vanished, and that strenuous attempts had been made to find and rescue him, to no avail.

The building of the bridge must have seemed a natural opportunity to the Mars boys looking for employment on their discharge from the ship, as it was for ex-Mars boy Walter White.

BRAVERY OF AN EX-MARS BOY

Walter, a boy of sixteen was engaged at the bridge (as a clayer) when a lamentable explosion occurred at pier 54 where he and others were blown into the river. The night was dark and stormy, but White was able to save himself by swimming to a boat moored nearby. Instantly he applied himself to the work of saving others, and he succeeded in rescuing three men, who must have perished. The Committee of the Humane Society expressed their 'great admiration of the signal bravery and presence of mind' displayed by the boy, and voted to him the highest reward which the Society bestows.

Walter, thirteen, and his younger brother Thomas, eleven, had both been admitted to the Mars in October 1869. Walter was described *as destitute and uncontrollable* and his parents Robert and Jane White were *in poor circumstances* at their home at Ferryport-on-Craig (Tayport). In 1872 he was *discharged to trade at Newport*, but his brother was not so fortunate; in his discharge section there is a short sentence which reads *4th September 1871, died at his home Tayport.*

Dealing with disease

Accidents, illness and disease were unfortunately commonplace in Scottish city life, and on the Mars Dr Stewart, the physician from Newport, had his work cut out dealing with his boy patients. Scarlet fever, or scarlatina, was a frequent problem.

SERIOUS OUTBREAK OF FEVER

Scarlet fever has broken out on board the training ship Mars, and had spread so rapidly among the boys, notwithstanding all precautions, that 22 are lying ill, and two have died. The Committee have deemed it advisable to remove the larger portion of the 300 boys on board the Mars, some being placed on board the tender Lightning and others in charge of respectable friends. The Committee have applied to the Dundee Police Commissioners for the use of the fever hospital, at present empty, to accommodate 100 of the boys, and the application was granted at once. It is suspected that the water used on board the Mars and obtained from the Newport side of the Tay, is unwholesome, and investigations are being made.

Bad as this was, the isolation of the ship from both shores meant that the boys managed to miss the worst epidemics that plagued Dundee. As we can see from this excerpt from the minute books, they were attempting to come to terms with 'certain realities'.

Captain Scott reported the death of John Thompson which occurred on the 5th July 1871, and referred to the doctor's report for particulars – this boy died after about four hours illness – the cause of death being congestion of the brain.

The meeting having had reference to the fact that now and again a sudden death had occurred among the boys similar to the present, was of the opinion that it would be proper in such cases to hold a post mortem examination. The meeting accordingly empowered Captain Scott in conjunction with Dr Stewart, to hold such an examination in any case where it appeared desirable, and for that purpose to call such assistance as might be deemed necessary.

Dr Stewart had asked for improvements to be made to the sick quarters on board ship and in 1884 he got more than his wish when, thanks to the good graces of Mrs Stewart of St Fort, the granary at Woodhaven was turned into a quite magnificent new hospital.

The Committee had to deal with many applications for assistance, from many quarters. Here are two quite different ones from ex-Mars boys.

7th May 1874, there was read a letter from John Harvey. The boy who in 1870 fell from aloft on board the Mars, and who until recently had received a weekly allowance from the Institution, asking further assistance. This application was carefully considered, and the Committee were of opinion that the case was now one of the Parochial Board, and that they would not be justified in making any further allowance.

The next is from 7 July 1881:

The Secretary represented that a boy named James McDonald, and [sic] been sent to sea 3 years ago had lost his right arm and in consequence had become destitute, that he, the Secretary, hoped to get McDonald appointed a telegraph message boy but that some clothing was necessary. The Secretary was authorized to give McDonald clothing to the value of £2 in the event of his obtaining suitable employment.

The Cardiff Home

James may have gone to sea from what was called the 'Cardiff Home', which had been established to assist boys who were waiting for berths to join the Merchant Marine. Initially, it had been set up using the Cardiff Sailors' Home, but that was found unsuitable, and in 1895 a permanent home was set up at 219 Penarth Road, Cardiff. One of the Mars staff, Mr Carr, who had formerly been Chief Officer on board the training brig *Francis Molison*, was appointed to superintend.

The account book for 1895 records:

So far this new shipping home has been an unqualified success. By means of it the Committee are enabled to exercise supervision and control over the 'Mars' boys up to the very point of their getting on board the vessels in which berths have been secured for them, not only so, but the home is open to them on exceedingly moderate terms when they return from a voyage, a privilege which seems much appreciated.

In 1896 no fewer than fifty boys were shipped from Cardiff on expiry of their time, which was half of the boys leaving the ship during that year.

The Cardiff Committee comprised local dignitaries and shipowners – Chairman Mr John Guthrie, Mr Albert Macintosh, the Rev. J. T. Wordsworth, Mr James Manuel, Mr William Mackenzie, Mr F. S. Tollputt, Mr B. T. Holtham, Mr James Hurman, Mr E. R. Moxey, Mr W. R. Corfield, Mr Phillip Turnbull and Mr R. H. Carrick.

A Mars anecdote

In a train crossing the Tay Bridge one day a little girl pointed to the Mars and asked what it was. 'That's the Mars,' replied her father. 'That's where you would have been if you'd been a wee laddie.'

Figure 13 The boys at Woodhaven Harbour under the command of Mr Flynn. The building behind is the old granary, which is being converted into a spacious hospital for the training ship.
(Dundee City Council Central Library)

5

Fire! Fire! Fire!

Because of the very nature of the ship's construction, the use of paraffin to light the vessel, and the presence on board of 300 troublesome boys (400 were permitted by 1880), the constant fire drills were not merely training exercises. There was a constant risk that the ship could be destroyed by fire, as others had been before. As early as 1876 there was a threat by boys from the Mars to set fire to the ship. On Thursday, 1 June 1876 the *Liverpool Mercury* carried this story:

> *There seems to be an epidemic of wickedness among what I may call our public children. The burning of the Goliath Training Ship was followed by what was generally believed to be the incendiary conflagration on board the Warspite, and that by a similar attempt at Falmouth. A few days ago we had the news of the attempt to sink the Caledonia at Devonport, and now today comes news of a conspiracy – to burn the Mars Training Ship at Dundee. Unhappily, crimes of this sort have a tendency to become an epidemic . . .*

The threat to burn the ship was made by some of the eleven boys who escaped from the Mars. The *Hampshire Telegraph* and *Surrey Chronicle* reported:

> *Eleven boys made a daring escape on Tuesday morning from the Mars Training Ship, stationed on the Tay. Between one and two o'clock they evaded the watch, lowered a boat kept ready in case of fire, and rowed ashore. Most of the runaways have since been captured, and they confess that if they had not succeeded in escaping they intended to set fire to the ship. A strict investigation is to be made regarding the escape.*

Though all the boys were recaptured and punished, stories circulated once again about the ship's management. The *Dundee Advertiser*, in a riposte to an article which had appeared in the *Daily Telegraph*, replied:

> *BOYS WILL BE BOYS*
>
> *. . . the repetition of which will sufficiently answer the Daily Telegraph in its suspicion that there must be something wrong in the management of Training Ships because the lads now and then try to run away from them or break out into acts of insubordination. So far as the Mars is concerned we doubt whether, taken as a whole and all the year round, there are 300 better behaved boys or 300 happier and more contented boys anywhere than these on board of her. It is also doubtful whether there are 300 boys of their class in schools on shore who receive so little*

punishment and have so many amusements provided for them. Nevertheless, do what you will, you cannot have 300 lads together without there being a few unruly and troublesome spirits amongst them, one or two of whom may devise pranks and tricks, and put mischief into the heads of others who, left to themselves, would never think of such things. Excellent, too, as the discipline of a ship is for 'licking into shape' the youngsters who go on board a training-ship, there is a certain monotony in it, and the spirit of adventure which is characteristic of lads fond of the sea naturally jumps at the idea of an attempt to escape, or even doing something to give all the boys a trip on shore. This, we believe, is the entire explanation of the conduct of the runaways during Captain Scott's brief absence in the tender Lightning *last week. There was nothing in it to cause any reflection on the excellent and excellently managed Mars Training Ship Institution.*

This seems to be a glowing tribute, but we must be aware that the newspaper's proprietor, Mr Leng, was a staunch supporter of the Mars, and he may have been swayed by his connections to it, or simply motivated by his intimate knowledge of, and confidence in, the institution.

There were other attempts made to set fires on board, but by far the most serious and most successful attempt was made in the early hours of Saturday, 28 May 1883, yet again in Captain Scott's absence. *The Scotsman* reported:

THE MARS TRAINING SHIP FIRE

Early on Saturday morning an alarming fire broke out on board the Mars Training Ship in the Tay, which resulted in the destruction of the Captain's quarters and the greater part of the stern of the vessel . . .

The vessel is under the charge of Captain Scott R.N., but he is at present on a cruise in the Mars tender with about 60 boys. The watch was set as usual on Friday night, and on Saturday morning about three o'clock he discovered smoke issuing from the poop-deck of the vessel. He aroused Mr Flynn, the chief officer, who at once broke open the cabin door, when he discovered that a serious fire had already taken hold of the place, and was making rapid progress. The fire bell was immediately rung, and in about five minutes thereafter every boy on board had turned out and was at his post. The ship's hoses were speedily attached, and in short time eleven hoses and six l'Extincteurs [sic] were being worked under the direction of Mr Flynn and the officers. It was soon apparent that, single-handed, the officers and boys could not cope with the fire, so firm a hold had it got; and as the appearances were of an alarming nature, the chief officer thought it prudent to send the majority of the boys on shore, leaving just sufficient on board to man the pumps. The lads were thereupon mustered, and they were ordered to collect their effects and prepare to leave the ship. Boats were got ready, and 250 boys left the ship in the most orderly manner, and were landed at Woodhaven Pier. The

87

steamer Elcho Castle *came alongside, followed by the* Iron King, Forfarshire, *and* Dundee. *The additional fire extinguishing apparatus thus brought to bear had not long been in operation before the men got at the seat of the fire, and very shortly thereafter the flames were got under. The damage is confined to the stern of the ship. The poop and captain's apartments, including bed-rooms, dining and drawing rooms, are completely destroyed, along with the furniture and fittings, and generally the whole of the stern is so much destroyed that it will need extensive repairs. Fortunately the ship's papers were saved.*

The origin of the fire is a mystery. Captain Scott's apartments were kept carefully locked during his absence. They were opened yesterday to allow the servants to clean the rooms preparatory to the return of Captain Scott, and when the servants left there was not the least trace of fire. It is believed that the loss will amount to at least £1,000.

Another article on the fire from the cuttings book in Newport adds the following information:

Meanwhile the fire had been observed at the Dundee side. Several of the dockgatemen had noticed smoke issuing from the Mars, and the Harbourmaster's attention having been called to the matter an alarm was raised . . .

Great praise is due to those who promptly responded to the summons for assistance. Ex-Provost Robertson, who got early intimation of the fire, was

quickly on the spot, and rendered invaluable aid and advice. Captain Yule, the Harbourmaster, accompanied by a number of dockgatemen, went across to the ship in the tug Fairweather, *and did efficient service in extinguishing the flames. Captain Methven and the crew of the* Dundee; *Captain David Edwards and the crew of the* Forfarshire; *Captain Legge and the crew of the* Iron King; *Captain Speed and the crew of the* Elcho Castle *(the latter being the first steamer to get alongside the Mars); and Mr Petit and the men of the* Unicorn *all gave most willing and valuable assistance.*

The prompt and efficient actions of Mr Flynn, the chief officer, along with the crew and the boys under his command, plus the ships which came to their aid, combined to save the ship and prevent loss of life. The investigation into the causes of the fire began, and on 5 July, at a special meeting on board, the minute reads:

Captain Scott further reported that boys Leonard, McGuiness and McDonald, the boys concerned in the recent fire, were taken to Cupar on the 30th, charged with breaking into the Captain's cabin and stealing certain articles. They were sentenced to 15 lashes each, 10 days imprisonment, and 5 years detention in a reformatory.

Figure 14 This photograph shows some of the boys taking part in boat drill with Chief Officer Flynn in charge.
(Dundee City Council Central Library)

The boys, who had been admitted from Fife, Galashiels and Glasgow, now faced a much stiffer sentence than they would have had upon the Mars and they may have regretted their moment of madness.

Mr Flynn, chief officer, the hero of the hour, deserves a special mention. An article of 1897 in praise of his gallantry describes him as a brave officer and hero of the Crimea:

> *Mr Flynn is the 'beau ideal' of a British navyman. Of active figure, alert features, fearless eyes, genial and courteous, he bears the stamp of a man who has learned what duty means, and where and when to expect obedience from others.*
>
> *[Mr Flynn entered the Navy in 1852] . . . He was present at the siege of Sebastopol, and, as showing the terrible cost in life to the British side, it may be mentioned that of the 1,000 men who entered action on board the ship [HMS Queen] with Mr Flynn, only 342 survived. Mr Flynn recollects that one of the midshipmen on board was the present General Sir Evelyn Wood. For his Crimean services Mr Flynn received the Crimean medal with the clasp for Sebastopol, together with the Turkish. He also wears the medal for long service. While on the China station he took part in a brush with Chinese pirates, when a number of the latter were killed. In this affair Mr Flynn was wounded. In 1874 Mr Flynn left the navy, time expired; and in the following year he came to the Mars, a step taken on the recommendation of the late Captain Scott. [Mr Flynn was chief officer on the Mars for eighteen years.] On several occasions Mr Flynn has been instrumental in saving life, and a handsome barometer hanging in the little hall of Holly Cottage, West Newport, serves as a memento of his latest act of humane service . . .*

Fine words for a brave officer who had undoubtedly prevented death and destruction on board the Mars Training Ship. The spectacular fire which caused the demise of Glasgow's training ship, Cumberland, on the Gareloch in February 1889 was a perfect example of the tragedy which could befall these wooden-walled ships.

Musical life on the Mars

Music was a diversion, and a major part of life, on board the Mars. It gave the boys involved a welcome break from the rigorous training aboard. It not only gave them time away, but the chance of a free feed. In many cases, food was the only payment to the boys; for performances on HMS *Unicorn* in 1904, 1905 and 1906 there are receipts for *Bandmaster of the Mars 5/-, and chocolate for band boys 10/-.* The ship had three bands – the brass band, the pipe band and the bugle band – the origins of which went back to the very first days on the Tay.

Alexander McDougall, the ship's carpenter, describes the history of the bands:

Figure 15 The Mars band has long been famous in Dundee, and though the members change frequently, the standard of performance is very high considering their youthfulness. This photograph, taken in 1908, shows the brass band. *(Dundee City Council Central Library)*

The first music we had was that supplied by a naval pensioner called Candy who came north with the Mars. He had a flute, and at prayers every morning in Captain Wake's cabin our music was Candy's flute. We then got some brass instruments and formed a band. Among the boys who afterwards joined the ship were some tinker lads who could play the bagpipes, and shortly after that we got a fife and drum band – so that we had no lack of music.

The first public appearance of the Mars bandsmen was at Edinburgh in 1872, and they gave such a good account of themselves that nearly all the Edinburgh boys wanted to come and join the Mars.

In 1877, on Saturday, 5 May, 260 boys of the Mars, including the band, were invited to Edinburgh, as *The Scotsman* relates:

On Saturday the young tars were up-betimes and, rigged out in full naval costume . . . they mustered outside [the Waverley Hall] *in processional order, with flying flags, and headed by their band, and accompanied by several members of the Local Committee, marched by the High School, round the Calton Hill, to the base of the Nelson Monument . . . After singing 'Rule, Britannia', which they did with great spirit, the lads next proceeded by way of Princes' Street and Hanover Street . . . and George Street, to the Albert Memorial, around which they formed a circle and, uncovering, played and sang with good effect the 'National Anthem'. . . . The processionists went up the Mound, en route to the*

Castle – a cheer being raised as they passed the Ramsay Lane Ragged School. With colours flying and band playing, the young blue-jackets marched round the Castle battlements and the Square – the soldiers turning out in considerable numbers to see them; and then by way of High Street returned to the Waverley Hall, where luncheon was served. Along the whole route traversed the boys were accompanied by crowds of people, the turn-out in Charlotte Square and the High Street being very large.

In the afternoon they played in front of an invited audience of 1,600 in Waverley Market, and the *working class* turned out in force for the evening concert, the number being between 6,000 and 7,000.

The band touring the country on the ship's tender was a powerful recruiting tool for the institution, as can be seen from an article in the *Glasgow Herald* in 1882:

THURSO – A CONCERT BY MARS BOYS

A performance of vocal and instrumental music was given on Saturday evening in the town hall, Thurso, by some 50 boys of the Mars Training Ship who are at present aboard the tender at Wick. The concert was hurriedly got up, but no sooner was the announcement made than the greatest enthusiasm was manifested to give the boys a generous welcome. Accordingly they were met at the train at 5 p.m. by an enthusiastic crowd and escorted to the hall, the youthful band playing appropriate airs. The chair was occupied by George Logan, Factor, who introduced the musicians. The manner in which the boys acquitted themselves elicited hearty applause. Mrs Hutton, wife of Major Hutton, of the Perthshire Militia, and Mrs Bremner, wife of Mr A. H. Bremner, assisted at the piano.

Singing was also a strong part of the curriculum and the ship's life, and for a time they had a quite outstanding teacher in Mr Frank Sharp, who was one of the leading exponents of the sol-fa method of teaching: Mr John Curwen, author of the sol-fa system, said, *in Dundee there were more children taught well in singing than in any other town in Britain.* On leaving the Mars, Mr Sharp in 1909 became the chief judge in the Leng medal competition, which was often won by Mars boys. Peter Milligan in 1916 won a gold medal for *a vigorous rendering of 'Up in the morning's no' for me'.* Other medal winners were John Orr, 1919; James Arthur, 1920; boy Murphy, 1922; James Gibbs, 1923; William Middleton, 1924; William Gregory, 1926; and Robert Jamieson, 1927. The singing instructor on board during this period of Leng medal success was Mr J. C. Fyfe, schoolmaster and noted singer, who was also a member of the *famous Dundee Select Choir.*

However, the next musical interlude became yet another test of Captain Scott's management skills, and would severely try his tolerance of stress.

Banned practice

The safety and security of the boys on board the Mars Training Ship seems to have been genuinely regarded as a very serious issue, so in March 1884, when a letter arrived on Captain Superintendent Scott's desk, little did he and the Committee imagine the effect its contents would have. It may be that Captain Scott thought that he could deal with the potential scandal quietly, in his own way, and in his own time, but he was soon to find out otherwise.

At a meeting held on board the Mars on 3 April 1884, the Mars minute book records that a letter was read from Captain Scott:

Dated 2nd April, representing that Mr Thomas, Head Schoolmaster, and Mr Stovin, one of his assistants, had without his [Captain Scott's] knowledge, taken evidence in writing from several boys in the ship in respect of grossly immoral conduct said to have been committed by Mr Butler, Bandmaster, and had handed said evidence to Captain Scott on Saturday the 29th March.

On receiving this document, to which Mr Flynn, Chief Officer of the Mars, had also appended his name, Captain Scott made inquiry into the matter and came to the conclusion that there were no grounds whatever for the allegations against Mr Butler.

A letter from Mr Butler, on the same subject, was read, and Captain Scott was requested to inform him that there was no complaint by the Committee against him and that he was free to resume his duties.

The Committee having heard Captain Scott and having considered the whole matter so far as laid before them, regretted to find that 3 of the principal officers of the ship should have so far, and in so censurable manner, exceeded the limits of their duty,

as to combine in taking evidence in so grave a matter, without the authority, or knowledge of the Captain Superintendent.

Under all the circumstances the Committee did not think it necessary to institute an enquiry in the matter, but they were unanimously of opinion that the services of the three officers concerned in it could no longer be retained. The Secretary was therefore instructed to inform Messrs. Thomas, Stovin and Flynn accordingly. At the same time he was authorized to pay to them whatever was due to them on the same being certified by Captain Scott.

This seems a harsh judgement on the three officers, who, at least on the surface, appeared to be acting for the good of the boys on board the ship. However, it did not end there:

A Special Meeting of the Executive Committee on board was called on the 18th of April where there was read a joint letter by Messrs. Flynn, Thomas and Stovin, recently officers on board the Mars, touching the matter for which their services had been dispensed with.

The letter led to a reconsideration of the circumstances which resulted in the discharging of these officers; and on the motion of the Chairman, it was agreed to hear them in defence of their contract.

Figure 16 The Mars crew with buttonholes.
(Fife Council Libraries and Museums)

They were heard accordingly, in the course of the questioning that ensued certain discrepancies as to matters of fact came out, and as it was found that these could be best cleared up on board the ship, the Chairman, Mr Walker, and Mr Robertson were appointed a Sub-Committee to act on board the Mars the following morning to make the necessary investigation, and report.

At least there now seemed to be a will to get to the heart of the matter, and not simply to hope that the problem would just go away. But were they looking for answers or scapegoats?

The investigation took place on 19 April and the sub-committee reported its findings at another Special Meeting on 23 April 1884:

At 10 a.m. on the 19th the investigation began. When I. Petrie, S. Instructor was examined . . . he gave evidence that Mr Stovin, 2nd Schoolmaster, had told him on Saturday 29th March, as a secret, that he had seen Mr Butler, the bandmaster, with 2 boys in his cabin who were abusing him. – The Committee also examined Mc Mahon [?] S. Instructor, who stated that on Sunday the 30th Stovin told him that he had seen Mr Butler standing in his cabin with his person exposed, and a boy standing in front of him.

The Committee also had before them A. McDougall, the carpenter, who stated that on Saturday the 29th March Mr Thomas, about 8 a.m., in his mess room showed him a paper with certain statements signed by boy A. Watt, by Mr Flynn, and

Mr Thomas and asked his advice. When Mr McDougall advised him to take it to the Captain, Mr Thomas said he would like to have clearer evidence before taking it to the Captain. Mr McDougall heard no more of it until the evening when Mr Thomas, and Mr Flynn, came to him. When they came in the evening both sides of the paper were written. They asked McDougall, whether they should lay it before Mr Butler with the view of letting him quietly leave the ship, and nothing would be known about it – or should he take it to the Captain. McDougall advised taking it to the Captain which was accordingly done. McDougall further stated that he believed Mr Thomas came to him with the view of getting at the truth and without any bad feeling against Mr Butler.

The Committee carefully, and anxiously considered this report, and the whole matter, and came to the unanimous conclusion that Mr Stovin had not been consistent in his statements relating to circumstances of a highly important nature; and therefore, that he should not be reinstated in the office he had held on board the Mars.

The Secretary was instructed to inform him accordingly, and authorized to settle with him by payment of a month's salary, and an equivalent for other allowances.

The cases of Mr Flynn, and Mr Thomas, were considered. The Committee resolved to re-instate these men in respective offices of Chief Officer, and Head Schoolmaster on board the Mars. But before doing that: that they appear before the Committee and be reprimanded for the breach of discipline of which they had been guilty, and that they apologize to the Committee and also to Captain Scott for the same. These officers were reprimanded accordingly; and at the same time they signed a paper in the following terms: Mr Flynn and Mr Thomas appeared before the Committee, and the decision to which the Committee had come in their cases having been read to them, they acknowledged their mistake in not having communicated, at once, to the Captain Superintendent of the Mars, the matters which came to their knowledge instead of taking evidence in regard to them and they here apologize both to the Committee and to Captain Scott for the error they had committed.

It seems strange, does it not, that with such seemingly damning evidence, Mr Stovin appears, at this point, to be the guilty party in the story? And what has become of the bandmaster? The minute dated 1 May sheds some light on the increasingly murky tale. At this meeting a letter was read from Mr Butler, referring to his previous letter, and stating that he was at once to leave the ship. Captain Scott was authorised to look out for a suitable man to fill the vacancy.

Yet again we have many loose ends and no satisfactory conclusion, with dismissals, reinstatements and investigations all adding fuel to the fire. All the ship's minutes were sent on to Colonel Inglis, the Government Inspector of Industrial Schools –

undoubtedly he had picked up on this controversy. At a meeting held on the Mars on 3 July, the Committee was made aware of his concerns:

The Chairman stated that Colonel Inglis had written to him and also the Secretary, requesting to see them concerning the recent differences among the officers of the Mars, and they had met with him, and Mr Rogers, on the subject. The Chairman also read a letter he had subsequently received from Colonel Inglis suggesting that the Committee should make a formal investigation into the grounds of these differences, and into the state of discipline generally on board the Mars, and to report to him the result. [Also at the same meeting there was read a letter from Mr Stovin] *late an Assistant Teacher in the Mars,* [asking] *to be re-instated in his former office. This was considered; and under all the circumstances the Committee resolved to authorize Captain Scott to restore Mr Stovin to his former position on board the Mars.*

Quite what was going on behind the scenes we can only surmise, but some official conclusion was necessary to end this problem. The appointment of Mr Gooding as bandmaster in place of Mr Butler seemed, at least, a small step in the right direction. The official investigation team reported their findings on 7 August 1884:

The Sub-Committee appointed at the last meeting to hold an inquiry on board the Mars touching certain of the officers, and also the state of discipline on board, gave in their report which was as follows:–

Your Committee went on board the Mars on Monday 7th July all the members being present. Also Captain Scott and it was agreed that he should have the right of asking any question of the witnesses, not objected by the Committee.

The Committee examined the following boys:

No. 97 Grattan: 3 years on board. Knows nothing wrong: any rumours to the contrary are false.

No. 397 S. Murray, nearly 16 years of age; was 16 months in the band; knows nothing of rumours – the boy Watt was a bad boy.

No. 379 John Collins, on board 3 years and 8 months – had heard rumours, and has himself told lies – Has no knowledge of anything wrong on board the Mars – was forced to make the charge by the Schoolmaster.

No. 171 C. Beach, Mess room boy. Have heard reports, don't believe them. Think they began with bad boys who had been reported against the bandmaster.

No. 182 C. Mitchell, nearly 16 years old, in band nearly 2 years, only once in the Bandmaster's cabin drying up water after storm. Knows nothing of the rumours.

Your Committee then called for the following Officers:

Mr Flynn: Has been nearly 9 years first officer in the Mars. Captain Scott has given strict orders for maintaining proper discipline in the ship and for preventing any immorality. – Only six months before this matter came up, Captain Scott had again drawn the attention of the officers to the subject. Admitted that he had no very friendly feeling towards the Bandmaster but considered him a good man for 'leering the boys'. It is a common thing for the boys to make unfounded charges against officers. Has known that many times. The boy Julius (otherwise Burns) was an extra bad boy. Never heard any bad reports, nor anything wrong in the ship till the Friday when I was called to be a witness to a statement against one. Asked as to the present discipline of the Mars? Said it continues good, and was of a high order considering the class of boy we have to deal with.

Mr Butler, the Bandmaster: The boy Watt began the rumours because I had punished him for faults. The boy Julius (Burns) was a dreadful bad boy. The Schoolmaster and I had quarrelled and he tried to injure me. Asked what was the cause of the quarrel said the Schoolmaster took offence because he shewed two visitors into the school master's cabin. Mr Flynn has also shewn me ill will. Said there was ill feeling among the boys towards Mr Flynn and Mr Thomas since the rumours arose . . .

It does seem a little odd that while the public position on the boys, given out by the staff and Committee members, was that they were unfortunate but honest, in this investigation they were portrayed as less than truthful and trustworthy.

Alexander McDougall, the carpenter, repeated his evidence from the last investigation, and the next to be interviewed was the schoolmaster:

Mr Thomas, Schoolmaster: was then called in and told that the boy Collins had said that he had been forced to make statements against Mr Butler by him – the Schoolmaster – Mr Thomas answered: I deny this, in no way did I try to influence him, on being asked as to the discipline of the Mars, he said it was good. That he personally knew of nothing amiss, as to the immoral practices in the ship, nor had he heard any rumours of such till the boy called on him on the Friday – Asked as to his present belief in the rumours, he said he had no such belief in the rumours. He said he had no such belief and did not know of anything amiss in the ship or in any officer.

From the evidence your Committee are of the opinion that the discipline of the Mars continues good, and there was no evidence whatever that any immorality had been practised.

Was this the Navy way? Now that the immediate problem had been dealt with, it no longer existed? Famously, looking through their blind eye? They seemed content to accept the status quo, and not to find out the truth of what had (allegedly) happened. The report concludes:

That Captain Scott had always been careful in giving such orders as to the position of the iron beds and hammocks of the boys that with good lights every boy might be seen to be in his own billet by the sentries in the sleeping decks. And further, that an additional night watchman had been appointed to the ship which would render it almost impossible that any wrong could take place – Besides Captain Scott had repeatedly given orders to the officers of the ship that no boys be permitted to enter their cabins.

Signed W. H. Maitland Dougall
George Halley
W. Y. Blyth Martin

I suppose we should not be surprised at the findings of these inquiries. To this day, investigating committees decide that if a problem no longer exists, there is no one to blame, no matter the damage done in the past.

As a final gesture to the seemingly innocent bandmaster (but more likely to draw a line under the whole affair), on 13 August 1884:

The Committee resolved to grant a certificate to Mr Butler. Who had left the ship in connection with the unfounded charges that had been brought against him. And to declare that in the opinion of the Committee borne out by the whole of the evidence Mr Butler had left the Institution without the slightest evidence against him.

Although Mr Butler, through his representative Mr Dickson, appealed for a more generous settlement to this affair, the tone of the reply from the Committee advised him to leave things as they were:

Dundee, 4th September 1884

There was read letters from Mr Butler, late Bandmaster of the Mars expressing dissatisfaction with the certificate of character sent to him; and the reply thereto by the Secretary was also read. The Committee were of the opinion that Mr Butler should be satisfied with what he had got, and declined to grant any other certificate.

So the matter ends, unsatisfactorily, except that a better and more watchful system of management had been put in place. Neither guilt nor innocence seems to have been proven, nor did they seem to have been an essential part of the inquiry.

In the midst of this debacle, there was another important visitor to the Mars, when on 16 April 1884 Lord Rosebery and party left the Edinburgh slip aboard the *Princess Louise* to pay a call upon the ship. Some of the other famous personages to honour the ship were the Duke and Duchess of Edinburgh in 1881, and the Marquis of Lorne in 1889; twenty-six Chief Constables visited in 1893, and there were many other distinguished guests. The Mars visitors' book must have made interesting reading. All these visitors were treated to a fine luncheon, but what of the boys, what were they to eat?

The Mars menu

The dietary scale for the ship in 1895 consisted of the following: each morning, *5oz (oatmeal) 1 pint of porridge and half a pint of milk*; for dinner, *1 pint of soup, pea or ox head, thickened with 1oz of rice, bread and a pudding*; and for supper, *1 pint cocoa with bread and treacle.*

The dietary scale for 1927 is a little different:

Weekdays: Breakfast – Porridge and milk with buttered roll.
Monday: Dinner – Rice pudding with Currants, Potatoes
             and Roll.
             Tea – Bread with Jam or Marmalade.
Tuesday: Dinner – Pea soup (Bacon), Potatoes and Roll.
             Tea – Cocoa and Coffee (alternatively), Bread
             and Butter.
Wednesday: Dinner – Irish Stew (Meat, Potatoes and
             Doughboys).
             Tea – Bread and Dripping.
Thursday: Dinner – Suet and Treacle Pudding (alternate
             weeks), Bread Pudding (Boiled) with Currants.
             Tea – Bread with Jam or Marmalade.
Friday: Dinner – Fish, Potatoes and Roll.
             Tea – Cocoa, Bread and Treacle.
Saturday: Dinner – Mutton Broth, Vegetables, Potatoes
             and Roll.
             Tea – Bread, Butter or Dripping.
Sunday: Breakfast – Cocoa, Bread and Butter.
             Dinner: Sea Pie (Meat, vegetables and Pie Crust).
             Tea – Bread and Jam.
Supper every day of the week: Roll.

The cost of these provisions had to be met by the ship's Committee, and at all times fundraising was pursued with vigour. From the smallest to the greatest donation, all were noted in the minute books. Here are just a few from April 1883:

Donations:

Boys' and Girls' Religious Association, Lochee, £1. 1/-

Mr J. W. Thoms, £1

Mayor, Inchyra, £2. 2/-

Mrs John Sharp, a supply of comforters, and from sundry others, periodicals

From the executors of the late Dr John Boyd Baxter, £100

Messrs. Baxter of Balgavies, £500

Mrs Molison, Errol, £2,000. This donation, being especially for the maintenance of the 'Francis Molison' tender

Oddly enough, this sum was not used as requested, but was invested in some wild and wonderful companies by the Committee:

£1,300 in the Matador Land and Cattle Company [a famous Dundee financial investment company], £500 in the Texas Land and Cattle Company, £500 in the Dundee Investment Company and £500 in the Dundee Mortgage Company.

In 1889 their investments took them to even more exotic places:

£400 with the Bank of Rio de Janeiro, £400 with Queensland Nat Bank, and £400 with the Bank of the River Plate.

In 1890 Mr Mess, the Mars's Secretary and Treasurer, reported

Figure 17 Three boys demonstrate their hammock technique in the ship's orlop deck.
(Dundee City Council Central Library)

that, as a result of a conference with Mr Currie, of Shiell and Small, regarding the question of the constitution of the institution, changes should be implemented. Part of their conclusion reads as follows:

The trustees ought to invest the funds on the securities permitted by law, such as inter alia:

Bonds and dispositions in security over heritable property

Debenture stock of any Incorporated Railway Company in Great Britain

Reference Guaranteed Lieu Annuity or Rent Charge stock.

Lucrative as the earlier investments may or may not have been, it was thought more prudent to invest in the future in British railway companies and lend money for land and property development, as they did for six tenements in Scott Street, Dundee. Investments in 1908 show a change of strategy:

£1,100 Midland Railway Company
16 shares, Arbroath and Forfar Railway Company
£500 Great Western Railway Company
£1,000 Great Central Railway Company.

The Mars fund still exists to this day. It is administered by Henderson Loggie, Dundee, and gives small grants for naval training. This comes from the fund's *Grant making policy and objectives*:

It shall be in the power of the governing body to award bursaries and grants to people of promise to enable them to attend courses in preparation or continuation of a seafaring career in any of its

branches. The governing body are required to maintain in good repair the war memorial erected at Woodhaven Pier, Wormit, by the subscription of the boys on board the 'Mars'.

A great financial benefactor who donated directly to the boys was Mr J. Lindsay Bennet, of London and St Andrews. He died in London in 1898:

For a long time he had been at the entire cost of providing numerous prizes to be distributed amongst the Mars boys for proficiency and good conduct in school . . . Until within the last three or four years Mr Lindsay Bennet made a point of being present at these functions . . .

Mr Lindsay Bennet, at an early period in his career became a Director of the Hudson [sic] Bay Company, London and assiduously attended to their most extensive commercial transactions in their offices in London. It was understood that these were of a very successful description, and that Mr Lindsay Bennet had amassed a large fortune.

When he became unwell in St Andrews, the boys from the Mars gathered in the street outside his residence, and heartily cheered him. His daughter carried on the tradition of attending prize-givings and donating prizes after his death.

6

A Grave Tale

Captain Scott, as can be seen from the investigations mentioned in Chapter 5, was under severe pressure in discharging his duties, possibly much more so than he would have been in a normal naval command. The spotlight was always on him, and the attendant administrative duties were proving arduous, and were eventually to take their toll.

DEATH OF CAPTAIN C. C. SCOTT

Dundee Advertiser, 30th December 1892

The public will learn with surprise, and the supporters of the Mars Training Ship Institution with deep regret, that Captain C. C. Scott, the Captain Superintendent of the Mars Training Ship, expired shortly after four o'clock yesterday afternoon at the cottage at Woodhaven.

. . . Captain Scott, accompanied by Mrs Scott, visited Brighton, Bournemouth, Portsmouth and Plymouth returning to the Mars about ten days ago. He had however, obtained little benefit from his brief holiday, and it was observed by those on board that he was looking far from well. On Monday he came

ashore to the Cottage at Woodhaven, to which he was quite able to walk, and although not strong was cheerful. Dr Stewart, his medical attendant, became anxious, however, about some alarming symptoms indicating serious derangement of the stomach, and at his suggestion Dr Bramwell came over from Edinburgh on Wednesday to a consultation, when Dr Stewart's apprehensions were confirmed. The alarming symptoms became more pronounced, great weakness supervened, and as already stated, death occurred yesterday between 4 and 5 p.m. Deceased was in his 66th year.

In the Mars minute book of 30 December 1892, the chairman explains

that he had called the meeting in consequence of the sudden and unexpected death of Captain Scott the Superintendent of the Mars. He gave an account of an interview which he had with Mrs Scott and some members of the family in connection with the funeral arrangements, and he desired to know whether the committee wished to give any directions or to express any views in regard to whether the funeral arrangements should be in naval order or otherwise. After some consideration the meeting requested the chairman to express to Mrs Scott the desire of the committee that provided the family had no objections they would like that the band of the Mars along with say 100 boys should form part of the procession from Craig Pier to the ceremony.

The *People's Journal* of 7 January 1893 carried an account of what the rest of Dundee's population experienced that New Year:

THE MIDNIGHT HOUR

The 'Happy New Year' and other greetings usual at the birth of another year were less frequently accompanied by the too common practise of 'passing the bottle', the pyrotechnic display also on the small scale. A squib spluttered here, a cracker there, and now and again a rocket shot upwards, illuminating the darkness for a brief spell, while a roman candle blazes forth from some third or fourth storey window. Under these conditions the boom of the gun at the barracks was heard, the steeple and St Paul's church bells rang out a merry peal, and the crowd, first raising a cheer of welcome to 1893, dispersed homewards or to the houses of friends to 'first fit', carrying with them bags of sweets, oranges and other seasonable gifts. Soon the streets were cleared of people and stands, the shops put up their shutters, and the policemen on their respective beats were alone left in possession. It may be mentioned that in the course of Saturday and yesterday about 60 persons were lodged in the police offices.

While the festivities were being enjoyed in Dundee, on the Mars the atmosphere would have been very sombre. On the day of Captain Scott's funeral, Tuesday, 3 January 1893, the *Advertiser* reported that the weather had been cold and frosty over the New Year holiday, and many workers in Dundee had not yet returned to work. The deserted city streets must have seemed eerily quiet. On the Tuesday fresh snow had been falling throughout the day: *the result was that the streets in the centre of Dundee rapidly became wet and slippery, and this together with the mud which adhered to footways caused walking to be attempted with considerable difficulty.*

The service in Newport

The funeral of Captain Scott, R.N., Superintendent of the Mars training ship, who died at his residence at Woodhaven on Thursday last, took place yesterday afternoon, the remains being interred at the Western Cemetery, Dundee.

From his position and long connection with Dundee, the deceased was well known, and the obsequies were consequently largely attended by all classes of the community. The remains were first conveyed in a hearse from Woodhaven to S. Mary's Episcopal Church, Newport, where a religious service was held at one o'clock. The Rev. S. B. Hodson and the Rev. W. S. Nicholson, S. Salvador's, Dundee, were the officiating clergymen, and there was a large attendance of the general public. The coffin, which was of oak, with heavy brass mountings, was covered in the Union Jack, and surmounted by a number of beautiful floral wreaths sent by the Mars boys, the officers of the Mars, Mr D. H. Littlejohn, Mrs Lennox Scott, Dr and Mrs Walter Scott, Tulse Hill, London; Mr and Mrs Mess, Dundee; Mrs Leng, Kinbrae; Mr and Mrs John A. Leng, Newport; Mrs Moir, Kilburn Bank, Newport; Miss Adie, Newport; Mrs James Adie, Thornbank, Dundee; Mr and Miss Morison Duncan of Naughton; Mr and Mrs John H. Walker of Westwood; Mr and Mrs William Walker, Newport. Placed in the chancel, the coffin bore the following inscription:–

Charles Casely Scott,
Staff-Commander, R.N.,
Captain Superintendent, Mars.
Born
21st February 1827
Died
28th December 1892

The service was that prescribed by the English Church, and was very impressive. It included the chanting by the choir of the familiar words, 'I am the Resurrection and the Life', and the singing of the hymn, 'Jesu, lover of my soul'. At the conclusion the coffin was borne out of the church, the Dead March being played the while on the organ. At the foot of the steps the cortege was formed. The hearse was preceded by the Mars Band and the officers of the ship, and was followed by the mourners, viz. – Mr A. L. Scott, Dr C. C. Scott, and Mr F. E. Scott sons; Mr Alexander Mackay, assessor, Thurso, brother-in-law; Mr D. H. Littlejohn, son-in-law; Master Charles Littlejohn, grandson; and ex-Provost Robertson. Following these were a number of the personal

friends of the deceased and a large body of the public, among others present being the Rev. Thomas Munn and the Rev. James Scotland. On the Tay Ferries Pier 100 boys from the ship were drawn up in two lines, between which the hearse and the company passed the band, which had been stationed at the top of the pier, playing the Dead March and 'When our hearts are bow'd with woe'. In Newport the procession was witnessed by most of the inhabitants, and several shopkeepers closed their places of business as it passed. Flags floated at half mast from the mansions in the burgh and from the flagstaffs at the Blyth Hall, the boatsheds, and the Mars Training Ship.

The large, solemn procession, which included city dignitaries, friends, colleagues, 100 Mars boys and the ship's band, followed by numerous horse-drawn carriages, made its way with some difficulty from Craig Pier, where the *Discovery* now is, up Union Street, on to the Nethergate, along the Perth Road and into the countryside, to the Western Cemetery, to pay their last respects to Captain Scott.

AT CRAIG PIER

. . . a large number of mourners waited the arrival of the body, while outside the streets were crowded by the general public. Shortly after two o'clock the Tay Ferries steamer drew alongside. The cortege was then re-formed, with the Mars Band in front, the boys immediately behind, then the hearse, with the officers of the ship walking on each side, followed by the chief mourners (including from his point Mr W. O. Dalgleish,

President of the Mars Training Ship Institution), the general company bringing up the rear in a long line of carriages. In this order the procession slowly wended its way to the cemetery, and all along the route, via Union Street, Nethergate, and Perth Road, it was witnessed by crowds. The band, with muffled drums, played the Dead March in 'Saul'. At the cemetery, the concluding part of the English Church service was conducted by the Rev. Mr Hodson, and at the close the band – which, along with the Mars boys, surrounded the grave – played the well known hymn, so appropriate on such sad occasions, 'When the heart is bow'd with woe'. [There follows a long list of those who attended the funeral, including many of the town's leading citizens.]

It may be mentioned that yesterday morning each boy on board the Mars received a leaflet, in which Mr A. L. Scott, eldest son of the deceased, stated that the reason the number of those to be permitted to attend the funeral was limited to 100 was the prevalence of sickness in Dundee. 'I know', he said, 'that every officer and boy in the ship would like to pay the last mark of respect to my father by following his body to the grave, and would like to show how deeply they feel the loss of the noble-minded gentleman who for the last 23 years has devoted his life to them.' That, however, for the reasons mentioned, was impossible.

I'll leave the last words to this poem from the *Piper o' Dundee*, April 1897:

IN MEMORIAM CAPTAIN SCOTT, R.N., THE MARS

Toll, toll the muffled bell
The ensign hang half-mast;
Bear to his bier our sad farewell –
Our chief's in port at last.

His bark, with grating keel
Has touched the shining strand,
And others now must take the wheel
He held with faithful hand.

No more on board the Mars
Shall ring his clear command;
Never again the little tars
Will grasp his friendly hand.

Courteous and kind was he
A sailor staunch and true;
No braver spirit ruled the sea
No kindlier donned the blue.

To ocean's furthest rim
The lads he reared have spread:
And many a manly eye will dim
To know the Captain's dead.

Then toll the muffled bell
The ensign hang half-mast
Bear on the bier a last farewell
To him whose soul has passed.

W. C. D.

We'll Send Ye Tae the Mars

On paying a visit to the Western Cemetery to see Captain Scott's grave – I had a map showing his last resting place – I was surprised to be confronted by a bare plot. There was no gravestone. It seems quite incredible that, after such a public expression of grief, there was no tombstone erected to the brave captain. It may have been damaged or vandalised, but there is no record of its existence, and no sign that there ever has been one. Yet there are five bodies in the plot; his daughter, Caroline Jessie Lennox, was the first to be buried there, dying of scarlet fever in Woodhaven at the age of thirty-five. One might imagine that, even if he were a modest man who did not want a grand monument to mark his grave, the rest of the family would have been recorded on a headstone.

The next Captain to be appointed to the ship was Lieutenant Augustus Lennox Scott, Captain C. C. Scott's son. He had been educated at Dundee High School, and like his father, he would be in command for over twenty years. Lieutenant Scott was thirty-six years of age when he took over the Mars:

He entered the Navy as a cadet on board H.M.S. Britannia in 1870. He was midshipman on H.M.S. Immoralite in the Flying Squadron from 1872 to 1877, during which period the ship visited every quarter of the globe, and also formed part of the fleet which accompanied the Prince of Wales to India in 1875. He was sub-lieutenant of H.M.S. Boadicea during the Zulu war (1879) and was present in action with the naval brigade at the destruction of the town of Batanga, on the west coast of Africa, and was with the naval brigade at the battles of Laing's Nek and Majuba Hill during the Boer War in 1881, for which

Figure 18 Lieutenant Augustus Lennox Scott, Captain Superintendent 1893–1919.
(Fife Council Libraries and Museums)

he has the South African Medal. He was Lieutenant of H.M.S. Beacon *at the bombardment of Alexandria, in July 1882, and during the Egyptian war, for which services he received the Egyptian Medal, the Alexandria Clasp, and the Khedive's Star. Lieutenant Scott subsequently served on the Channel Islands station and in . . . H.M.'s training cruiser in the Mediterranean.*

He joined the Mars on the same conditions that his father had enjoyed:

He was in receipt of a salary of £400 per annum. He further received an annual allowance of £10 as against his expenses in extending hospitality to visitors to the Institution. He received the free use of the cottage at Woodhaven. He had the privilege of using for his table any vegetables, flowers, fruits etc. grown in the garden at Woodhaven.

He was provided with free heat and lighting at the expense of the Committee.

Augustus Scott was to be Captain Superintendent for twenty-six years, and thanks to the work done by his father, he was to have a more stable captaincy. Yet the times were changing, and the question was, could the young captain, and the training ship, adapt to the changes? A speech made by Sir John Leng, MP, proprietor of the Leng Press, at a meeting to publish the ship's annual report in February 1906, looks back at the changes and forward to the challenges that lie ahead:

The first was the greater attention to manual instruction consequent on the almost entire replacement of sailing by steam navigation. The sailor, who had always been a handy man, had now to be even handier than ever. In the Royal Navy he was required to be half sailor, half engineer. The same was becoming more and more true of the merchant marine. What a different appearance our docks in Dundee have from 50 years ago! Then, at this season, they were crowded with Baltic brigs and coasting schooners, smacks and sloops, with a considerable number of whalers and a few square rigged ships and barques. Almost all these have disappeared. Brigs, schooners, and small craft all gone! Masts had gone, yards had gone, gaffs, booms, and spars had all gone, and with them the sails – square sails, lower, gallant, royal, sky scrapers, gibs, and fore and aft sails – all had gone. Remembering how picturesque, what beautiful objects, vessels in full sail often were, he lamented the change so far as the appearance of our ships was concerned. He lamented it still more from the change that had occurred in the crews. The old fashioned, thorough-bred seamen were fast passing away, their places being rapidly taken by what old sailors would call mere 'land-lubbers'.

Figure 19 This photograph, taken in 1902, shows the 'skeleton' crew left to man the Mars while the ship's company was attending annual camp at Elie. The 'old salt' with the magnificent moustache and beard, in the front row (left), is ship's carpenter Mr Alexander McDougall. The instructors in the second row are (from left): David Leslie (tailor), Wm. Taylor (boatman), Alex Bruce, Mr Dryden and Richard Burn (joiner).
(Fife Council Libraries and Museums)

When there were no sails, sailors of the old type were not required. Mere deck hands, cooks, stewards, filled up the crew in addition to a few navigators, the engineers and stokers doing the most important part of the work . . .

The emphasis in Sir John Leng's speech was intentionally focused on the Mars workshop training. Since its introduction as an experiment two years before, it had become a mainstay of the boys' training with the opening of brand-new workshops at Woodhaven in 1911.

TECHNICAL TRAINING AT THE MARS

Things seen are mightier than things heard, and a visit to the workshops in connection with the Mars Training Ship will do more than many words to convey an adequate idea of the great educative and reforming work which is being carried out at our doors.

. . . On five afternoons a week, in the building close to Woodhaven pier, a contingent of about 200 boys may be seen at work learning the rudiments of the carpenter's craft. Mr Richard Burn, the superintendent of technical training (ably assisted by Mr William Bowman, while the metalwork is in charge of Mr Haines), takes a genuine pride in showing the workshop to visitors and explaining

what the boys are doing. Some of them are busy shaping stools or turning candle sticks, some engrossed in the fascinating manufacture of dogs and cows and even elephants with wonderful tails that move their heads. Others prepare the inlaid work which goes to the fashioning of those beautiful trays and tables which are characteristically Mars products, while others still are only yet to discover how much wood is required to make a door three feet wide and eight feet high – a process during which a lad often for the first time perceives the practical possibilities of the multiplication table!

. . . A fair-sized showroom is fitted with specimens of the boys' handicraft. Most noticeable is an elaborate white wood spiral staircase with elegantly-turned pillars supporting the banisters; while a model door opening on hinges stands side by side with a tiny window which goes up and down . . .

. . . During the last few weeks of the year unusual animation pervades the scene, for all the boys with homes to go to visit their parents at this season, and they are allowed to carry as a present some specimen of their skill . . .

One of the many innovations in the workshops was that under the movable floor of the large main hall was a swimming bath. It was dug out of solid rock, and was 60ft by 20ft by 8ft at the deep end, and 4ft deep at the shallow end.

Figure 20 Instructor William Bowman stands proudly by his boys with their handiwork outside the workshops at Woodhaven Harbour. The arched building, far left, is still standing.
(Fife Council Libraries and Museums)

THE MARS SCHOOL ROOM

Here perhaps is the most thankless part of the work on board the Mars, for the boys' training and experience previous to admission do not tend towards scholarship or book learning. All the more praiseworthy is the enthusiasm of the different teachers. Mr Macbeth, the Chief Schoolmaster, points out with quick appreciation the brightest of his pupils, or explains sympathetically the presence of a big boy in the lowest class. Before we leave the school quarters Mr J. C. Fyfe, himself a singer well reputed, marshals his choir and puts them through 'The Bay of Biscay, O!' This musical training forms a practical, as well as popular, part of their education. The Mars band, under Mr Edward Nugent, is a great favourite, and there are few sweeter sounds than the strains of its music borne across the water on a summer evening. Such instruction affords a ready means of entering the army or navy in after life, it enables boys who go to shore occupation to become members of town and volunteer bands.

In the tailoring and shoemaking departments we found boys variously engaged in basting braid on blue collars, working a sewing machine, or cobbling boots. Captain Scott's aim is to model the boys on the British Bluejacket, the handy man who is good at most things.

In the kitchen we were shown a huge cauldron where the cocoa for the evening meal was being prepared. This is week-day fare, tea being allowed only on Sunday. Appetising little loaves, specially split up and spread with marmalade.

MARS ENTERTAINMENT

The hold of the ship serves as a gymnasium, where on the horizontal bar, the 'horse' and other appliances, the undergrown bodies of the lads get a chance of developing. The ambulance class under Mr James Anderson is a splendid feature in physical training. Here too, the social gatherings are held. Captain Scott, alive to the dangers which beset a Mars boy's life, gratefully acknowledges the services of the kind friends who relieve the monotony of the long winter evenings by frequent entertainments. He and his wife give gracious welcome to those who come to sing, exhibit lantern slides, or perform conjuring tricks to the boys.

Figures on previous pages

Figure 21 Two young Mars boys posing beside the staircase made in the workshop.
(Fife Council Libraries and Museums)

Figure 22 Mars boys at work in the workshop east room at Woodhaven.
(Dundee Art Galleries and Museums)

Figure 23 *(opposite)* This shows the boys 'off-duty' during their summer break at Elie, and is in striking contrast to the stiff, regimented, formal photographs normally associated with the Mars boys.
(Dundee Art Galleries and Museums)

The article goes on to describe and discuss the changes in the laws under the Children's Act, and concludes:

Since the passing of the Children's Act the percentage of Roman Catholics among the Mars boys has perceptively increased. The Mars, be it noted, is the only training ship at which Roman Catholics are received.

In the summer the boys go for a cruise on the brig 'Francis Molison' or to Elie for 5 or 6 weeks, where they sleep in hammocks and enjoy all the pleasures of camping out. [In 1902 the boys had the luxury of staying in the old granary on the pier at Elie, courtesy of Mr Baird, at Elie House. In good weather, they would march there and back, saving the expense of a train.]

The healthiness of the life on board is amply testified by the low percentage of sickness. On the afternoon when we visited the ship the large hospital at the water's edge was empty. But when any of the boys are ill they are tended by the medical officers Dr Stewart and Dr Rust, and the matron, with a care and tenderness which must be a new experience for most of them.

The idea to which the Captain Superintendent laughingly referred, that 'the Mars is a prison and the boys chained up at night', does not need to be exploded in this neighbourhood. It is a home where from the moment that they enter it all the influences make for good. When they come in, as some of them

do, at the age of 11, they are stunted, underfed, and underdeveloped both in body and in mind. Until they leave at 16 no effort has been spared to make the best of them, to educate their heads and their hearts, and by training them in the right use of their hands to make it impossible that they should ever join the deplorable army of the unskilled and the unemployable.

The increased percentage of Roman Catholics on the Mars mentioned in the article was partially due to an especially large number of boys who came from Glasgow. An arrangement was therefore made with the Mars's Glasgow agent. The minute book of April 1894 records:

Proposed Agreement referred to for the Glasgow Agent.

The Agent will have a general supervision of all boys from Glasgow and district, also Greenock and Paisley. He will keep a look out on them when they are on leave and after discharge and be ready to give them advice if necessary. He will forward to the Captain Superintendent not later than the 25th May and 25th November every year the address and occupation of all the boys in the district who have been discharged

Figure 24 Four Mars boys beside the model of a rowing boat, built in the workshops, with the aid of William Bowman, ex-Mars boy and now instructor, who looks on.
(Fife Council Libraries and Museums)

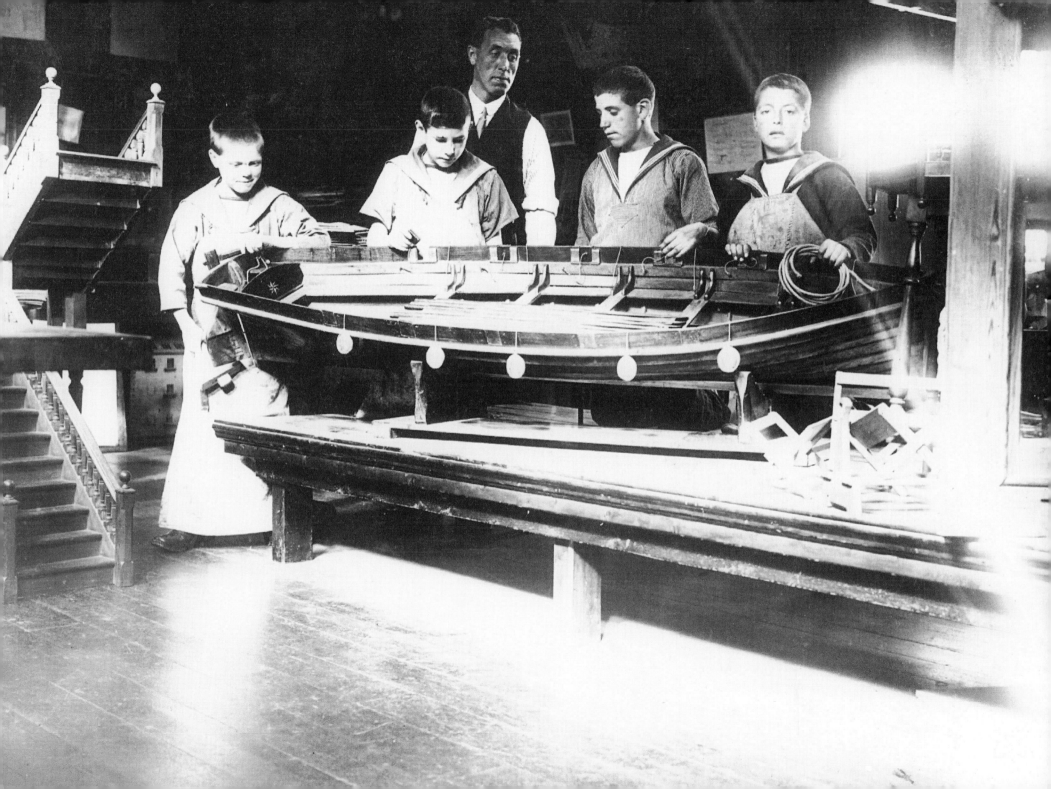

from the Mars during the previous four years. A list of the boys being supplied to him. This will be one of the most important parts of his duty and no trouble must be spared to obtain full, absolutely authentic, information.

He will attend at the court and do his best to keep up a steady supply of new boys, taking care that none are sent who are not suitable for a sea life.

His emoluments will be as follows: 5/- for each boy committed. £5 in May and £5 in November, after the Captain Superintendent has received and approved of his reports on discharged boys. £1 a year will be allowed for stationery. There will be no allowance for travelling expenses when on ship duty outside the suburbs of Glasgow.

Also in the same minute is recorded the resignation of Mr West, representative of the institution in Glasgow, and a recommendation to appoint Mr Stewart, agent for the Catholic School in Glasgow, for the month.

This agreement may have seemed a good idea at the time, but owing to the large number of boys now coming from the west coast, a change was made in October 1895:

It was resolved in future to discontinue making to the Glasgow Agent any capitation payment for his services in the commitment of boys, and in the opinion of the committee fairly remunerate him for his trouble last year.

The decision to discontinue the capitation allowance to the Glasgow agent may have had something to do with the figures: between 1894 and 1929 there were 61 boys admitted from Aberdeen, 545 from Dundee, 598 from Edinburgh and 1,239 from Glasgow.

A letter written by an ex-Mars boy from Glasgow is preserved in the ship's Annual Accounts:

Glasgow, 18th January 1899

Captain Scott,

Dear Sir, – Having a holiday on New Year Monday, I was walking over Albert Bridge, when I saw a little lad in naval uniform, the sight of which awakened my childhood days within me. I asked him, 'Where from?' 'Mars, sir,' was the answer. Proud was I to hear it. After asking for old friends and all about the old ship, and giving him an invitation up to my house before he went away from Glasgow, 'By-the-bye,' said he, 'I was told if I seen any old ship lads to get their address.' So I now take the opportunity of writing, after an absence of nearly fourteen years. I am not a lad now, but a man with a small family around me. I look back with joy on the three years that I spent on board the Mars, and to-day, thinking as a man, I thank God for having raised up such a noble Institution. Why, let me ask myself a question? In 1882 I was left an orphan – no brother or sister, no father or mother – in a great city like Glasgow. It was a lone position, not to speak of the temptations of sin abounding all around. I had a desire to go to sea. I went and seen Mr West, the agent for the Mars, and was accepted. I was put in the Fourth Class in School, worked myself up to the Advanced First; spent some time learning shoemaking under Mr Tibbet and Mr Dodds, which I turn into profit now, not a pair of boots going out of the house for repairing. I was for a time messroom boy for Mr Flynn and Mr Thomas. My two seasons on the Francis Molison were a delight to me. I obtained from Captain McNabb a certificate for excellence in seamanship and rowing, the first ever given to a boy from the brig. With joy I recall the life on board the ship. How, after a hard day's work was over, we would all go ashore to Wormit Bay, play at cricket, football, and all sorts of games. Then when all was over, we would march back to the ship singing, 'We had no cares on our heads, happy day.' Then would come the invitation out to our dear old friend's estate, Scotscraig, Admiral Dougall's. None enjoyed the rabbit hunt so much as he. There we would all be seated on the lawn getting our share of bread and jelly and a large measure of gooseberries. Then races and all kinds of sports. All over, we would march back, headed by our band, and each boy who had been successful in the rabbit hunt carrying a prize over his shoulder. The scene just now passes before me. No thought for the morrow. We were happy. When I read of his death [Admiral Dougall's] in the Glasgow Citizen, I said to myself, the Mars lads have lost a good friend. O, that there were a few more of his kind in principle and spirit. Soon after that I heard of dear old Captain Scott's death. This came as a stunner to me. They had lost a friend in one; but in the latter they had lost a father. May his mantle have fallen on you, like the Prophet of old, that you shall have the same grace from God to rule the boys. When my time was up I went to sea, and continued going till I got married. Being a cook, I got work in the wholesale provision trade, and with the education I received on board the Mars, developed into commerce, I find myself to-day, after hard work stage after stage, a commercial traveller, with a happy home, four bright children, and a loving wife – 'Heaven on earth'. This is the answer to the question – Had it not been for the Mars Training Ship, and good, practical advice taken from it, and the grace of our Heavenly Father, ten to one but I would have been numbered with the submerged class, or something worse. Kindly remember me to Mr Thomas, Mr Flynn, Mr Stovens, and all the other old officers. Trusting to see the old ship again, and to hear from you, I remain yours truly.

Unfortunately, the author's name was not recorded, but the writer's sentiments for the institution seem to be genuinely and warmly felt. Another ex-Mars boy's letter from the same source illustrates how and why Mars boys ended up in every corner of the world:

*U.S. Steamer 'Dexter',
New Bedford, Mass., U.S.A.,
Wednesday, Oct. 5, 1898.
Captain Scott,*

Dear Sir, – I now take the pleasure of writing you a few lines to let you know of our whereabouts. I am speaking for myself now and also John M., No. 73. We both left the ship in 1894; sailed on the German Bark '—' for Martinique, West Indies; from thence to Wilmington, North Carolina, where the vessel was run on shore. We lost everything we had, and were saved with the assistance of the life-saving crew on Baldhead Island, where we went on shore. John is on the U.S. revenue cutter '—' as Bugler, and I am Quartermaster on the above-named, so I thought you had lost track of us, so I just wrote this in the middle watch to let you know, and I must conclude by saying that the 'Mars' Training Ship is where I spent some of the happiest days of my life, but did not know it at the time. Please forward my Register Papers, which I left there.

P.S. – I have met several of the boys from there [the Mars] *in Boston and New York City, and they all join me in saying they wish they had the same days over again. I can assure you that neither John nor I had done anything yet that the 'Mars' need be ashamed of us, for we are doing exceedingly well, and have a great many friends over here . . .*

This is once again unsigned, but is yet another touching tribute. Some boys had greater adventures than others, as this letter from an old boy recalls:

Victoria, British Columbia, 12th October 1894

. . . Dear Sirs, I wish you a long and joyous life, to instruct and send forth into the world the boys who are lucky enough to be left in your care. When I myself left the 'Mars' I went into the merchant service and I made three journeys to sea. During that time I learned to be a good seaman. I also learned navigation enough to pass for mate, and at the termination of my fourth voyage I intended to try; but as luck would have it, I took a ship from Glasgow to British Columbia, and when we arrived there the country was in great excitement over some important discoveries of gold, which induced me to desert and join the throng then rushing to the fields. I stayed away two years in the interior of British Columbia. During which time I cleared about six hundred pounds sterling washing out gold dust. Then the drift that I was working on commenced to pan out, so that we were not making very good wages, on consideration that we were paying very high prices for our provisions. So we abandoned the claim, and I came down to Victoria, and I bought four acres of land two miles from the city, then I went to work on the steamer 'Beaver' belonging to the Hudson Bay Company, engaged in carrying miners and prospecting to the Corsair Mines. As I was making eight pounds a month in her, and as I liked the water better than the land, I determined to stay. I remained by her one year, and then I joined a schooner trading with the natives on the Vancouver coast for skins. I was mate of this vessel, and I liked the business very well, and if I was a passed man I am sure I have good prospects of getting a vessel of my own to go into this business, so I have determined to try and pass for a certificate . . .

Another old Mars boy, Murdoch McLeod, whom we have met before, joined the ship as a voluntary boy in 1869. The *People's Journal* carried an interview with him while he visited Dundee in 1939. On his discharge from the ship, he joined the Navy, then the merchant service, working his way around the world. After many dangerous and exciting adventures, including ten years in the China trade, working on China clippers, he eventually found himself in Australia:

When still a young man, Captain McLeod left the paths of the Trade Winds for the troubled seas of commerce. He became associated ultimately with the important firm of Gillespie Bros., flour millers, and after 40 years in business retired . . .

He built himself a little house at Manly, outside Sydney . . . and there, when not globe-trotting, he can, as he says, 'sit and see the sun rise in the east and set in the west'.

On the nomination of the Honourable Company of Master Mariners he was granted the freedom of the City of London for services rendered to the Mercantile Marine, and was also made a Liveryman of London, which carries with it ancient rights and privileges.

McLeod, of the China Clippers, takes pride in the possession of his 'ticket' for the captains' room at Lloyds. With that humility which is his endearing charm he is still prouder of having been number one boy on H.M.S. Mars in the 70's.

A wonderful tale, and a tribute to the institution that fed, clothed and educated him.

Stories abound of the various jobs the 'inmates' eventually took. One became a prosperous New York businessman; another a flight lieutenant in the RAF; another a doctor.

Dundonian Edward Hill, another ex-Mars boy, speaking to the *Evening Telegraph* in 1979, described the discipline on board:

Eddie is indebted to the discipline and education he received during his five-year 'break from the land'. 'The staff were very nice, but very hard,' he recalled. 'I learned a lot in the classes, but, more importantly, I also learned not to get into trouble . . .'

A report by Her Majesty's Inspectors in 1914 mentions the records of conduct kept by the ship:

Three records of conduct are kept, one by the Captain Superintendent, of serious offences, one by the Chief Officer, of breaches of discipline, &c., and one by the head schoolmaster, of faults committed in the school room. None of these lists is long, and except for two cases of absconding and a few of petty pilfering, the offences are not of a serious nature. These records and the bright and manly manner and bearing of the lads reflect the ease with which discipline is maintained, and the spirit which animates both officers and boys . . .

The parents of all the boys are visited frequently, and, if it is thought desirable in the interests of the boys' future lives, they are consulted as to their children's disposal on leaving. They may visit the ship once a quarter, and they write home every fortnight if they feel inclined to do so, and if they have stamps or money to buy them sent by their friends.

An interesting note from the Annual Report for 1902 gives a slightly different slant to the encouragement given to the boys to communicate with 'home':

Captain's report, boy's correspondence, number of letters passed through my hands by boys during year 1902 – 4,435. Despatched – 6,132. All the above letters passed through my hands, being duly entered in books kept for the purpose; content of letters despatched perused and corrected; stamps and monies enclosed in letters received are entered to the boys credit in the 'ship's bank.

I dare say that the inspection of outgoing mail was not only to correct spelling and grammar!

The Great War

The saddest and most monumental thing to happen during the command of Captain Superintendent A. L. Scott was the death of so many Mars boys during the First World War. The *Dundee Advertiser* of 26 February 1915 carried this story:

THE MARS

400 Old Boys at the Front
Remarkable Record

. . . A list has been prepared by the Captain Superintendent of boys from the Mars now serving in

the Army and Navy, and the list included 400 names. Special attention was drawn to one of these lads, William Sloan, 18 years of age, who went down in H.M.S. Monmouth, and to Lance Corporal Walter Cairns, of the Scottish Rifles, aged 21, who took command of a party of his regiment after all the officers had been disabled, and fought a very gallant rear action, for which he was awarded a medal for distinguished conduct. For the emulation and encouragement of the boys the Committees had caused to be placed in the ship an oak shield commemorating this gallant conduct.

In the account books for year ending 1919 there is a list published of 170 boys who died. Here are ten from the Honour List: *. . . killed in action on land and sea, also drowned at sea in consequence of being torpedoed, mined, etc.*

35 Sergeant Thomas Thorburn, Argyll and Sutherlands, DCM (and the Fourth Class of the Russian Order of St George)

168 Corporal Ronald Macdonald, Black Watch, MM

371 Quartermaster – Sergeant Walter Cairns, Scottish Rifles, DCM

174 Corporal James Beveridge, Scottish Rifles, DCM

306 Sergeant Calder, Royal Scots, MM

166 Corporal William Brock, 2nd Royal Scots, MM

116 Sergeant William Logan, DCM (two bars), Mons Star, Russian Order of St George, 4th Class. William was born in 1894 and admitted to the Mars in 1907. His father lived in *New Kirk Style, Dundee and he*

worked as a general dealer. His discharge, on 18 January 1910, was to the *Catholic boys' home in Edinburgh* and *in 1913 his address was c/o Mrs Minnocks, 11 the Cottages, Balgonie Terrace, Cardenden, here he was employed as a coal miner at Bowhill colliery.*

335 Sergeant George Seivwright, Black Watch, Messina Medallist, DCM. George's mother and father lived in the *Hilltown, he was discharged from the Mars on the 9th February 1904 to H.M.S.* Caledonia.

218 William G. Williamson, 1/4th Gordons. *Recommended for gallant conduct in the field by his Colonel in 1915. Specially mentioned in despatches.* William was committed on board from the court in Aberdeen *by Magistrate William Alan in 1909. He was born in 1896 and on discharge returned to the family home at 2 Gilcomston Place, Aberdeen.* On 23 November 1915 his occupation is given as *Drummer, Gordon Highlanders, 3rd Division, British Expeditionary Forces.* The last addition to his record reads *recommended for gallant conduct in the field July 1915.*

41 Corporal William Newall, RSF, MM. William, *born 7th January 1897,* was committed to the ship through the *Edinburgh School Board in 1909,* his mother, Mary, was a *charwoman* and her address given as *Simpson's Court, Greenside, Edinburgh,* although on his discharge his address is given as *c/o Duff, 94 Pleasance, Edinburgh.* The last entry in his discharge report is *that he died of wounds 1st of July.*

The official list concludes: *While the List has been compiled with as much care as possible it cannot be complete. Only those names, amongst a considerable number reported, about which there was no doubt have been included.*

In the *Evening Telegraph* of 1 August 1917:

TRIBUTE TO THE MARS BOYS

I had a talk last night (writes a London Scot from Dundee in the Advertiser) with a captain in the West Highland Regiment, who is at present on leave from France after two years in parts where the fighting has been at its fiercest. He was unaware of my association with Tayside – he himself is an Argyllshire man – when he said, 'All my men are splendid, of course, but many of my best fighters come from the East coast – from Dundee and some of the most determined of them are boys from the Training Ship Mars.

'Obviously life on the Mars works a world of wonders. The Mars lads are self-reliant, their discipline is perfect, and they are demons of resourcefulness.'

At the outset of the war, arrangements were made for the safety of the boys on board. The minute book of 13 August 1914 records that the *Chairman made a statement to the meeting with regard to the possibility of an attack on the Mars by destroyers or other war vessels during the present International troubles.* The boys were to sleep in the workshops until further notice. They were also to be kept busy helping the war effort, assisting the local branch of the Vegetable Supply Committee. *A weekly consignment averaging over 5 cwt. has since the beginning of September been collected by the boys and forwarded by rail to Aberdeen in crates made in the workshops. A thousand hand-sewn mail bags of large size are also being made in the shops for the Mediterranean Expeditionary Force.*

MARS TRAINING SHIP AND WAR MEMORIAL

Figure 25 This postcard of the old ship gives an accurate geographical fix to the mooring of the ship. It was taken after the building of the Celtic cross, erected to the memory of the Mars boys who fell in the First World War. The memorial was unveiled by Principal J. Yule Mackay, University College, on 21 April 1921.
(Fife Council Libraries and Museums)

On 21 April 1921, the War Memorial to the old Mars boys who fell in the Great War was unveiled by Principal J. Yule Mackay of University College, at Woodhaven. The whole cost of the memorial, which takes the form of a Celtic cross, was subscribed by the boys past and present.

The generosity and charity shown by the boys of the Mars was not taken for granted, and was noted in a report of a meeting of Dundee's Relief Committee (for the poor and unemployed) in 1909:

DUNDEE RIVAL CHARITIES

Relief Committee to be Wound Up
State of the Unemployed

The Committee of Dundee has agreed to stop operations, not because there are no unemployed in the city, there are believed to be about 15,000 people suffering through want of work – but because the funds are exhausted, and no more money is coming in. This decision was come to at a meeting of the Committee last night, presided over by Lord Provost Urquhart.

Mr W. M. Burke, the City Chamberlain, stated that the income up to Saturday last was £2,290 10s. 7d., and the expenditure £2,611 9s., leaving a debit balance of £320 18s. 5d. He had since got £110 from the Mars Band concert, and he expected £60 or £70 from the Sunday evening concert. There were also some accounts yet to be paid.

In 1919, two events were to mark the changes in the Mars experience. The *Courier and Advertiser* of 4 March reports:

SALE OF MARS TENDER FRANCIS MOLISON

May Become a Whaler

The brig Francis Molison, *the sailing tender of the Mars Training Ship, has been sold to Messrs. James Allison and Sons, Ship Chandlers &c., Dock Street, Dundee.*

. . . It is the intention of the trustees later on to acquire another vessel to be used for a similar purpose. The new owners of the Francis Molison *are, it is understood, to employ her in the Arctic trade, and she may, it is stated, be utilised as a whaler.*

The magnificent tender was never replaced, and that element of the boys' training had gone. The other crucial event was Captain Superintendent Augustus Lennox Scott's retiral due to ill health. He had been aware of changing attitudes to this type of training, and a letter from the Dundee University Archive from Patrick Geddes, the Professor of Botany who became famous as a traveller, writer and educationalist, to a colleague, J. T. Ewen, highlights the outgoing Captain's fears. Dated 9 June 1919, Geddes invites Ewen to visit the Mars before Captain Scott *who is very anxious about his life work leaves it. There is hope that the Scottish Education Department may take it over from the Admiralty.*

At the annual meeting held on Thursday, 29 May 1919, the next, and last, Captain of the ship was introduced:

. . . Captain (Commander) H. R. Heathcote R.N., who had entered the Navy in 1887 and had been a Commander of destroyers. Henry Ralph Heathcote has had a long and varied experience in the Navy.

NEW SUPERINTENDENT OF MARS

Figure 26 Captain Henry Ralph Heathcote, RN, Captain Superintendent 1919–29.
(Fife Council Libraries and Museums)

Formerly connected with the coastguard, he has been on active service since the outbreak of war, and has been particularly identified with the examination service in Queenstown. Early in his naval career he took part in quelling a Samoan rising, and for the duties to which he has now been appointed Commander, Heathcote will bring to bear the valuable experience he gained in the training of boys during the two years he served on the training ship Black Prince. Commander Heathcote's grandfather, grandmother and one of his uncles were killed in the Indian mutiny.

At the Annual Report meeting in April 1920, the sea change ebbing against the institution was being charted by Captain Heathcote, who mentions that:

. . . at the present moment the Mars Ship was passing from the Home Office to the Scottish Education Department which includes certain perplexities, but I venture to say that under this new office we should prosper.

Mr William Mackenzie, addressing the meeting on the subject of falling admissions, comments:

. . . all Industrial Schools are suffering in this way just now, and I heard from the Home Office that they had closed up a number of these schools in England on this account. All the Scottish schools are in the same position. I think it is this so-called 'probation' that is absorbing the children. The figures I have seen from London are that during two years 5,500 children were charged, 1,700 were sent to Industrial Schools and 3,800 were relegated to the tender mercies of probation. I do not know what happened to the 3,800, but speaking generally I feel sure that they are now on a much inferior platform in every way to the 1,700 who went to Industrial Schools.

For the time being, life was to go on, and the Mars boys very soon made more newspaper headlines, under the new Captain, when they saved the life of a pilot, Lieutenant Herbert Beardsworth, who crashed his aeroplane while attempting to fly under the Rail Bridge over the Tay:

Lieut. Beardsworth, of the R.A.F. at Leuchars, is undoubtedly one of fortune's favourites. Yesterday he had the thrilling experience of taking a header into the Tay from a crashing aeroplane, and was only rescued from drowning in the nick of time by a boat from the Mars, yet he was able, some hours later, to wave a cheery good-bye to the Dundee Royal Infirmary, where he had been taken, smiling all over none the worse for his dip. His bus, however, lies under the waters of the Firth.

The accident took place about half-past eleven in the forenoon, and a little to the west of the Tay Bridge. A coterie of seven 'planes had been treating the city to a fine exhibition of stunt flying for about half an hour, as a sort of foretaste of the display to be given next week in connection with the Joy Loan Campaign. Lieut. Beardsworth, one of the 'stunters', was attempting to 'shoot' the Tay Bridge from the up-river side, when his engine failed, and he found himself going straight for the water. As quick as lightning, he freed himself, and jumped clear just as his machine crashed into the waves, turned over and sank to the bottom.

Fortunately, however, Mr Wm. Taylor, third officer on board the Mars Training Ship, noticed the accident while occupied in his room. He ordered a boat away, and in a creditably short space of time a crew of twelve rescuers were pulling towards the struggling airman. They were none too soon, and the officer was lifted aboard in a state of exhaustion, after being in the water for about ten minutes . . .

[Lieutenant Beardsworth said] 'I was trying to go under the bridge . . . when the engine cut out. It all happened so suddenly that I just found myself in the water. I had to swim and splash about for a matter of ten minutes, but these boys from the Mars did very well indeed – in fact, they ought to get some sort of reward.'

The systems now established aboard the Mars would change little from now until the end of the institution in 1929. Experiments in farm work in Ireland had begun under Captain A. L. Scott and had proved successful. In 1903 it was reported that

he had visited North Ireland where a number of boys had been put out to farm service under arrangements made by Mr Stuart, the Glasgow agent of the Mars. Captain Scott found that the boys were doing well,

and the local police gave them a good character . . . The farms are small averaging 15 acres. The life is extremely suitable for boys of poor physique, the work being light, and the food plentiful, milk being a large element of the diet. The prospect of the boys being able to settle down permanently in Ireland is not encouraging. No wages are being paid during the first year and only £3 during the second; maximum wage of a farm labourer is £11 per year with board and lodging. Most of the male population of the district who do not own farms migrate to America as soon as they are grown up, and no doubt the Mars boys will do the same . . .

Another experiment was in the mining industry in Wales, and by 1913 Mars boys were working in the coalfields of South Wales. The Aberbargoed Valley, near Cardiff, was to be home to forty-five boys, working as miners' apprentices.

Changing social and industrial trends were negating the primary role of the ship. Many kinds of employment were taken up by the boys in 1921:

The total number of boys discharged in 1919–20–21, was 307. Occupation – 11 to Army bands, 32 Army, 18 Navy, 10 Royal Air Force, 41 Mercantile Marine, 3 Fishing, Total 115.

Figure 27   Captain Heathcote, RN, family, crew, dog and 400 Mars boys on board, 1925/26.
(Dundee City Archive)

Shore employment – 26 Miners, 28 Iron and Steel Trades, 11 Farm Service, 9 Railway Service, 5 Tramway Service, 20 Mill and Factory Workers, 8 Machinists, 7 Warehousemen, 12 Carters, 12 Dockyard and Foundry Labourers, 9 Carpenters, 3 each to Brewery Work, Blacksmiths, Shoemakers, Painters, Shop Assistants, 2 Firemen, 2 Bakers, 2 Butchers, 1 Tailor, 1 Slater, 1 Printer, 8 to Casual Occupations and 4 in Borstal and 1 in Prison. Total 299.

At the account meeting for 1921 Captain Heathcote mentions some of the year's highlights, but also a chilling statistic:

January 22nd, by invitation with 250 boys I visited The Savoy Cinema and saw the Prince of Wales Colonial Tour.

October 7th, 210 boys attended the Kinnaird Hall by invitation, and witness the film 'Pollyanna'.

Report on boys discharged in 1919–20–21.

Total number discharged 307.

Of this number deduct 5 who died while under detention.

I can make no comment on this quite startling fact, hidden amongst a lot of other facts and figures; the minute books of the time add little in the way of enlightenment.

By 1922 the end seemed almost inevitable for training ships, and the choice in Scotland came down to which of the two ships, the Mars or Glasgow's Empress, would go first. The *Dundee Advertiser* of 30 December 1922 notes:

FIGHT TO RETAIN MARS

Awaiting Decision of Department

The Mars training ship, that picturesque old vessel that has rested at her moorings on the Tay for the last 50 years, may have to go as a result of the economy measures of the Scottish Education Department, to be abandoned [sic]. Since both [the Mars and the Empress] are under complement at present one is considered sufficient. Conferences have been held between the respective committees of the two ships and the Department, and the claims to survival of each examined, and now the momentous decision considered by the Department.

Whichever ship is left – and the claims of the Mars are based on National grounds as compared with the rather more parochial [sic] of the Empress – it will have the distinction of being the last of its kind in the United Kingdom, for the English craft were put out of commission some years ago.

The *Glasgow Herald* on Tuesday, 13 February 1923 carried the bad news for the Empress:

Considerable surprise and disappointment have been caused in the West of Scotland by the announcement that, for reasons of National Economy, the Clyde Training Ship 'Empress' is about to be closed down. Since the Clyde Training Ship Association took over the 'Cumberland', the predecessor of the 'Empress', in 1869 over 6,000 boys have under gone training, mainly in Seamanship on the pleasant waters of Gareloch.

In July, only twenty-seven boys were transferred to the Mars from the Empress.

Captain Heathcote had fought a brave rearguard action on behalf of the ship, but the days were numbered for floating Training Institutions. His attempt to raise the profile saw the Mars band appearing in front of Dame Nellie Melba at a fête in Kirkcaldy in 1925. In these modern times new methods were used to spread the Mars message. Newspaper adverts were placed:

Mars Training Ship Institution (Industrial School), Newport, Fife. Finely situated on the Firth of Tay.

Ship licensed to carry 400 – 30 per cent, of present inmates are Voluntary cases. Boys trained for entry into the Navy, Army, Mercantile Marine, and Shore Occupations. Formation of Character.

Land Establishment of Manual Workshops (Carpentry, Tailoring, Smithy, &c.), Swimming Bath, Recreation Ground, Hospital, Special Shipping Home at Cardiff.

On 26 September 1925 the Mars Choir broadcast from Dundee under conductor James C. Fyfe. The programme consisted of:

Unison song, 'Danny Boy' (Traditional); Part Song, 'Hail to the Chief' (Bishop); Negro Spiritual, 'Steal Away' (Fisk Singers); Unison Song, 'I Passed by Your Window' (Brahe); Part Song, 'Hundred Pipers' (Lady Nairne); Part Song, 'Logie Buchan' (Halket).

Captain Heathcote himself made radio appeals for funds for the Mars from Glasgow and Dundee radio stations in December 1927. The Dundee broadcast was under the umbrella of 'This Week's Good Cause'.

The changes in law regarding juvenile crime, the growth and scope of the Scottish Education Department, and the lack of boys being committed to the ship, all compounded their misery. The lack of new recruits to the ship introduced strange bedfellows. In its last years, possibly for the first time, the Mars took in 'juvenile delinquents' along with their usual admissions of homeless and destitute boys, and there was a growing number of voluntary boys.

The last boy to be admitted to the Mars was Alexander Taylor Campbell, ship number 22, registration number 6562, sentenced at Stirling Police Court on 22 February 1929.

The last straw was the condition of the ship herself, and an Admiralty inspection sealed her fate, as reported by the *Courier and Advertiser* of 13 April 1929:

FUTURE OF MARS TRAINING SHIP

. . . Mr Slater Brown stated that as a result of a survey of the ship that had been made the Admiralty could not grant a certificate of safety. Because of this the Scottish Education Department decided to withdraw the whole of the committed boys and transfer them to land Industrial Schools, leaving only the voluntary boys to be provided for.

At 6.30 a.m. on 27 June 1929, the last acts were beginning to be played out. The *Dundee Evening Telegraph* describes the scene at Woodhaven:

. . . the old Mars was not allowed to go unheralded and unsung. As we watched her pass the harbour the note of a siren from one of the ships there reached us across the water; then another, and another, and another, and a little tug, which resembled nothing more than a cocksure little boy drawing an outsize wooden horse, returned the compliment.

The *Courier and Advertiser* reports:

No funeral pomp and circumstance attended the passing of the Training Ship Mars from the Tay yesterday.

In the grey of the morning the powerful tug Bullger, belonging to the Leith Towage and Salvage Company, steamed into the estuary.

At 6.30 she ran alongside the old training ship.

By eight o'clock all preparations for departure were complete, the signal given, and in tow of the Bullger the Mars set out down the river on her last journey.

It was a silent procession. 'Not a drum was heard, not a funeral note', not even a farewell was said . . .

Figure 28 The final day of the Mars at Woodhaven, 27 June 1929: the tug *Bullger* begins to take the strain, and the sad procession to the breakers' yard at Inverkeithing begins.
(D. C. Thomson, Dundee)

ELIE'S REGRET

It was with feelings of sadness that the people of Elie and Earlsferry saw the passing of the Mars far out on the waters of the Firth of Forth [on her way to Inverkeithing] *. . .*

Yesterday, in saying 'Goodbye', the Mars seemed to want to efface herself as much as possible. At times behind a screen of smoke from the tugs, as if she were acutely conscious of her ignominious position of being towed up the Forth to the shipbreaker's yard . . . The Mars completed the voyage to Inverkeithing shortly after 6 o'clock, and was safely berthed at the shipbreaking yard of Messrs. T. W. Ward and Sons, Sheffield.

A moving and sad tale, but the ship was not quite finished yet. There was one more act of defiance from these wooden walls:

DEFIES THE ART OF THE SHIPBREAKER

The demolition of the old training ship Mars, which lay so long moored at Wormit-on-Tay, near Dundee, is proving a stiff proposition to the shipbreakers, Messrs. Thomas W. Ward & Co., at their Inverkeithing yard. Her massive oak timbers vary from eight inches to over two feet in thickness. So far, she has been shorn only of masts, bowsprit, super-structure, and top deck, and in the time occupied in doing that work the breakers have been accustomed to demolish two modern-built liners. 'Breaking up steel ships is child's play to this work,' said a

shipbreaker; 'only now can I fully understand the pride of bygone mariners in the "Hearts of Oak".'

. . . Explosives are being employed to blow asunder the stronger part of the old ship.

So hard and seasoned with age are her massive sides, that an attempt to drive a three-inch nail resulted in the nail bending over rather than entering the vessel's side. It is estimated that the Mars contained between 3,000 and 4,000 tons of solid timber. She carried 300 tons of cast iron as ballast.

At Woodhaven Pier, an auction was held to dispose of the ship's stock and equipment over three days, including desks, and gymnasium, hospital and cookhouse equipment. At Curr and Dewar's auction rooms, Ward Road, the bedding, wearing apparel, and the band instruments were sold. Thankfully, many of the Mars brass band instruments were purchased for use on HMS *Unicorn*; some are still in use today.

The Scotsman of Thursday, 27 June 1929 records a few interesting postscripts:

PASSING OF THE MARS

Fruitless efforts have been exerted to resuscitate the Mars Institution in the form of a nautical school ashore. On the score of economy the Scottish Education Department decline their further support. The cost of providing a suitable building could be met, but the substantial sum needed as an endowment in order to establish the school, with its subsequent upkeep, on a solid foundation has been unobtainable. The boys having been disposed of variously, the ship was evacuated on June 1st, taken over by the Admiralty, and sold. To-day for the first time within sixty years, there is a blank in the once familiar spot on the Tay . . . A reminder of what has been achieved in the past will be the figurehead of the Mars which it is proposed to erect on shore adjacent to the boys' War Memorial, facing the river where the old ship lay so long, exerting a noble endeavour on behalf of the youth of Scotland.

The Mars Shipping Home at Cardiff will be continued for a time with the purpose of maintaining the after-care of her seafaring lads.

Whatever did happen to the figurehead?

Let us leave the last word to Mr J. C. Fyfe, the teacher of English and music on board the ship from 1907 to its end, who on the morning of the leaving of the Mars, watched from the harbour at Woodhaven, and wrote this touching account:

A group of us stood on the shore smoking contemplatively as we watched the workmen burn through the thick chain cables. The tug started off, and then, slowly, almost imperceptibly, the great

Figure 29 This is the sad demise of the Mars Training Ship. So solid was her construction that explosives had to be used on certain parts of the ship to break her up. A tragic and poignant end for such a mighty vessel. *(D. C. Thomson, Dundee)*

unwieldy ship swung round and made her way down the estuary of the Tay.

It was the last voyage of the Mars. We continued to watch her until she disappeared behind the projection on which stands East Newport. It was June 1929. She had lain out from Woodhaven since 1869, and now she had gone . . .

The Mars had been a landmark – if such an expression be permitted – familiar to two generations. Now she had gone to the shipbreakers. For those of us to whom she had been a 'home from home' there was, inevitably, a certain poignancy in watching her slow progress down the Tay.

So there we stood, making no comment, uttering no valedictory speeches. We saw her out of sight, and we – smoked . . .

The stories yet to be told are of the great successes and failures and everyday adventures of the Mars boys: that's for another book, perhaps 'Sons of the Mars'?